AQA
GCSE
History

# ELIZABETHAN ENGLAND

## c1568–1603

**Wesley Royle**

DYNAMIC LEARNING

HODDER EDUCATION
AN HACHETTE UK COMPANY

The Publishers would like to thank the following for permission to reproduce copyright material.

**Photo credits**

**p.9** © UniversalImagesGroup/Getty Images; **p.10** © Universal History Archive / Universal Images Group/REX Shutterstock; **p.11** *t* © World History Archive/Alamy Stock Photo, *b* © Print Collector/Hulton Fine Art Collection/Getty Images; **p.12** © GL Archive/Alamy Stock Photo; **p.13** © World History Archive/Alamy Stock Photo; **p.14** *t* © ACTIVE MUSEUM/Alamy Stock Photo, *b* © Mary Evans/The National Archives, London. England; **p.15** © Frank Walker / Alamy Stock Photo; **p.16** © Dea Picture Library/Getty Images; **p.18** © World History Archive / Alamy; **p.21** *tl* © The Print Collector/Corbis, *bl* © ACTIVE MUSEUM/ Alamy Stock Photo, *tr* © Universal History Archive/Getty Images, *br* © Granger, NYC. / Alamy Stock Photo; **p.23** © FALKENSTEINFOTO/ Alamy Stock Photo; **p.25** © Heritage Image Partnership Ltd/Alamy Stock Photo; **p.26** © TopFoto; **p.32** *l* © eye35.pix/Alamy Stock Photo, *r* © Pawel Libera Images/Alamy Stock Photo; **p.33** © john hill/Alamy Stock Photo; **p.34** © The Art Archive/Alamy Stock Photo; **p.37** *t* © John Morrison/Alamy Stock Photo, *b* © Ian Dagnall/Alamy Stock Photo; **p.40** *l* © GL Archive/Alamy Stock Photo, *r* © GL Archive/Alamy Stock Photo; **p.42** © The Art Archive/Alamy Stock Photo; **p.43** *br* © World History Archive/Alamy Stock Photo, *tr* © PAINTING/Alamy Stock Photo, *bl* © World History Archive/Alamy Stock Photo, *tl* © World History Archive/Alamy Stock Photo; **p.45** © Fotosearch/Stringer/ Archive Photos/Getty Images; **p.47** *c* © Hulton Archive/Getty Images, *b* © Timewatch Images/Alamy Stock Photo; **p.48** © mizio1970/123rf; **p.49** © A Rich Man Spurns a Ragged Beggar, from 'A Christall Glass of Christian Reformation' by Stephen Bateman, 1569 (woodcut) (b/w photo), English School, (16th century) / Private Collection / Bridgeman Images; **p.53** © Lebrecht Music and Arts Photo Library/ Alamy Stock Photo; **p.55** © World History Archive / Alamy Stock Photo; **p.57** *r* © GL Archive/Alamy Stock Photo, *l* © World History Archive/Alamy Stock Photo; **p.59** *l* and *r* © World History Archive/ Alamy Stock Photo; **p.60** ©The Granger Collection/TopFoto; **p.63** *tl* © Arcaid Images/Alamy Stock Photo, *bl* © Andreas von Einsiedel/Corbis, *tr* © Tracey Whitefoot/Alamy Stock Photo, *br* © The National Trust Photolibrary/Alamy; **p.65** © Vintage Book Collection/Alamy Stock Photo; **p.67** The Pope's Bull against the Queen in 1570 (engraving) (b&w photo), Hulsen, Friedrich van (c.1580-1660)/Private Collection/ Bridgeman Images; **p.68** © The National Trust Photolibrary/Alamy Stock Photo; **p.69** The Trial of Edmund Campion, illustration from 'Ecclesiae Anglicane Trophea', 1584 (engraving), Cavalieri, (Cavalleriis) Giovanni Battista de' (c.1525-1601)/By permission of the Governors of Stonyhurst College/Bridgeman Images; **p.72** © 2003 Topham Picturepoint; **p.73** © Pictorial Press Ltd/Alamy Stock Photo; **p.76** © Mary Evans/The National Archives, London, England; **p.79** © Granger, NYC/Alamy Stock Photo; **p.81** Portrait of Philip II (mounted on a cow), the Duke of Alencon, the Duke of Alba, William of Orange and Queen Elizabeth I, Moro, Philip (d.1578)/Private Collection/ Bridgeman Images; **p.85** © Hulton Archive/Getty Images; **p.86** and **p.64** © Archivart/Alamy Stock Photo; **p.88** © Jon Lewis/Alamy Stock Photo; **p.89** © British Library/Robana/REX/Shutterstock.

**Acknowledgements**

**p.12**, **p.17**, **p.20** (Sources 6 and 8), **p.23** (Source 12), **p.28**, **p.38**, **p.45** (Sources 3 and 4), **p.49** (Source 13), **p.50** (Source 14), **p.69**, **p.75** (Source 5), **p.82** (Source 4), **p.83** (Sources 6 and 7), **p.85** (Source 10), **p.89** (Sources 2 and 3) all from Harmsworth, A., *SHP Elizabethan England: A Study in Depth*, Hodder Education (Dubai, 2015); **p.15**, **p.20** (Source 5), **p.27** (Sources 6 and 8), **p.45** (Source 2), **p.66**, **p.67** (Sources 5 and 6), **p.68** (Sources 9 and 10), **p.70** (Sources 14 and 16), **p.77** (Source 10), **p.85** (Source 13) all from Mervyn, B., *The Reign of Elizabeth: England 1558–1603*, Hodder Education (Croydon, 2015); **p.20** (Source 7), **p.49** (Source 10), **p.67** (Source 3), **p.70** (Sources 13 and 15), **p.74** (**Source 3**) all from Anderson, A. and Imperato, T., *An Introduction to Tudor England 1485–1603*, Hodder Education (2001).

The wording and sentence structure of some written sources have been adapted and simplified to make them accessible to all pupils, while faithfully preserving the sense of the original.

Every effort has been made to trace all copyright holders, but if any have been inadvertently overlooked, the Publishers will be pleased to make the necessary arrangements at the first opportunity.

Although every effort has been made to ensure that website addresses are correct at time of going to press, Hodder Education cannot be held responsible for the content of any website mentioned in this book. It is sometimes possible to find a relocated web page by typing in the address of the home page for a website in the URL window of your browser.

Hachette UK's policy is to use papers that are natural, renewable and recyclable products and made from wood grown in sustainable forests. The logging and manufacturing processes are expected to conform to the environmental regulations of the country of origin.

Orders: please contact Bookpoint Ltd, 130 Milton Park, Abingdon, Oxon OX14 4SE. Telephone: +44 (0)1235 827720. Fax: +44 (0)1235 400454. Email education@bookpoint.co.uk Lines are open from 9 a.m. to 5 p.m., Monday to Saturday, with a 24-hour message answering service. You can also order through our website: www. hoddereducation.co.uk

ISBN: 9781471864292

© Wesley Royle 2016

First published in 2016 by

Hodder Education,
An Hachette UK Company
Carmelite House
50 Victoria Embankment
London EC4Y 0DZ

www.hoddereducation.co.uk

Impression number   10 9 8 7 6 5 4 3 2 1

Year           2020  2019  2018  2017  2016

Cover photo © Getty Images/DEA/G. DAGLI ORTI

Illustrations by DC Graphic Design Ltd, Cartoon Studio Ltd. and Oxford Designers and Illustrators

Typeset in ITC Giovanni Std Book 9.5/12pt by DC Graphic Design Ltd.

Printed in Italy

A catalogue record for this title is available from the British Library.

# CONTENTS

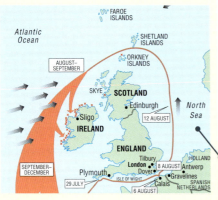

## It will help you to learn the content

Is your main worry when you prepare for an exam that you won't know enough to answer the questions? Many people feel that way. And it is true you will need good knowledge of the main events and the detail to do well in this British depth study. This book will help you acquire both the overview and the detail.

The **text** explains all the key content clearly and comprehensively. It helps you understand each period and each topic, and the themes that connect the topics.

We use lots of **diagrams**, **maps** and **figures** to help you to visualise, understand and remember topics. We also encourage you to draw your own diagrams – that is an even better way to learn.

### SOURCE 4

Thomas Becon, a Norfolk clergyman, in 1554.

*Thou hast set to rule over us a woman, whom nature hath formed to be in subjection to man… Ah, Lord, to take away the empire from a man and give it to a woman seemeth to be an evident token of thine anger towards us Englishmen.*

This book is full of brilliant **sources**. This course deals with some big issues but sources can help pin those issues down. History is at its best when you can see what real people said, did, wrote, sang, watched, laughed about, cried over and got upset about. Sources can really help you to understand the story better and remember it because they help you to see the events and ideas in terms of what they meant to people at the time.

### THINK

1   Why do you think such harsh punishments existed for vagrants?

Throughout the book there are tasks which are designed to build your understanding of a period or issue step by step. **Think** questions direct you to the things you should be noticing or thinking about. They also practise the kinds of analytical skills that you need to improve in history and they will help prepare you for the **Focus Tasks** – see opposite.

### KEYWORDS

Make sure you know what these words mean and are able to use them confidently in your own writing. See the glossary on page 94 for definitions.

- Circumnavigation
- Colony
- Empire
- Galleon
- Nationalism
- New World
- Ottoman Empire
- Printing press
- Privateers
- Renaissance

**Keywords**. Every subject and topic has its own vocabulary. If you don't know what these words mean you won't be able to write about the subject. So, for each topic we have provided a keywords list. These are the kinds of words or terms that could be used in sources or in an exam question without any explanation, so you should aim to understand them and use them confidently in your writing. They are all defined in the **glossary** on page 94. But we also want you to create your own keywords list – write down each word with your own definitions.

### TOPIC SUMMARY

**Elizabeth's background and**
- The Tudors were a relatively new dynast Elizabeth's grandfather at the end of the
- Elizabeth's father, Henry VIII, had broke Ann<s> <s>lvn

Finally there is a **Topic Summary** at the end of every topic. This condenses all the content into a few points, which should help you to get your bearings in even the most complicated content. Some people say it is good to read that summary before you even start the topic to know where you are heading. Associated with each summary is a **Tip** that suggests where you should start when revising this topic.

# It will help you to apply what you learn

The second big aim of this book is to help you apply what you learn, which means to help you think deeply about the content and develop your own judgements about the issues, and make sure you can support those judgements with evidence and relevant knowledge. This is not an easy task. You will not suddenly develop this skill. You need to practise studying an issue, deciding what you think, and then selecting from all that you know the points that are really relevant to your argument. One of the most important skills in history is the ability to select, organise and deploy (use) knowledge to answer a particular question.

The main way we help you with this is through the **Focus Tasks**. These are the big tasks that appear at the start and end of each topic. They bring together your learning and help you turn it into something memorable and creative. Focus Task A (at the start of each Topic) helps you make notes and gather information as you read; Focus Task B (at the end of each Topic) gets you to use your notes to analyse what you have learned and complete some written work. We have tried to make this work interesting and creative rather than giving you an essay or exam question every time but there are also Practice questions as well. Both stages are important – gathering and organising the information and using it to show your understanding of it.

## FOCUS TASK A

### Elizabethan culture

Complete a table like this using the information on pages 34–44.

| Aspect | Summary of developments | Key people (and details) | Key places (and details) | What this aspect says about Elizabethan England |
|---|---|---|---|---|
| Architecture | | | | |
| Fashion | | | | |
| Theatre | | | | |

## FOCUS TASK B

### The 'Golden Age'

You have been compiling a table about culture in Elizabethan England.

1  Which aspect of culture do you think saw the most significant developments? Explain your choice.
2  'The Elizabethan Age was a cultural 'Golden Age'. How far do you agree with this statement? Write a balanced answer using evidence from your table.
3  Use your table to write a travel guide for travellers visiting Elizabethan England.
   - Point out the must-see cultural highlights. Give background information and practical advice about how best to enjoy the sights and sounds of the Elizabethan world.
   - There might also be certain dangers to warn the tourists of in order to keep them as safe as possible.
   - Pictures, maps and diagrams would be useful.

# It will help you to prepare for your examination

If you read all the text and tackle all the Focus Tasks in this book you will find you are well prepared for the challenges that exams present, but you will probably also want something more exam-focused – you will want to see the kinds of questions you will face in an exam and how you might go about answering them.

Practice Questions are provided at the end of each topic to help you develop your skills.

**Review** at the end of each chapter explains the aims of each question type and helps you practice the skills which can be useful to answer them.

**Assessment Focus** on page 90 takes you through each question type and provides sample answers and comments so you can see what a possible answer might look like.

## REVIEW of Chapter 2

### Life in Elizabethan times

Here is another opportunity to review your learning using You will be set FOUR questions on the British depth study.

Question 1 will be on interpretations. The interpretation cou written source. For example:

## ASSESSMENT FOCUS

### Elizabethan England c1568–1603

How the British depth studies will be assessed

The British Depth Studies will be examined in Paper 2. All Studies will be on the same paper so make sure you pick th questions could be on any part of the content so you need

# Introduction

## A few things you need to know before you start

### England and Wales

- **Ruled over by the Tudors** from 1485, after a long period of civil war known as the Wars of the Roses.
- **The monarch** had a lot of power, but there was also a parliament and the nobility were powerful, too. Government became far more BUREAUCRATIC and modern in this period.
- **The Church** was rich and powerful, but it lost its political independence after England underwent a REFORMATION when it broke away from the Catholic Church in the 1530s. The Church became state-controlled and the power of the monarchy grew as a result.
- As part of the **English Reformation**, the monasteries were dissolved in the 1530s. This led to a huge rebellion in the North called the Pilgrimage of Grace.
- The break with Rome was followed by a lot of religious confusion and **deep divisions** between Catholics and Protestants.
- At the start of the sixteenth century, there were about 2.7 million people living in the country. The **population** had risen to over 4 million by the end of the Tudor period. Most people lived in the south east of England.
- **Woollen cloth** was England's most important industry and export product.
- **About 9/10 of people lived in rural areas** and most worked the land. The growing trend was to enclose the land so it could be used for sheep farming rather than growing crops.
- There were **a few towns**, such as York and Norwich, but they were small by modern standards, only containing a few thousand inhabitants. London was the most important settlement and its population quadrupled in the sixteenth century, to about 200,000 people.
- **Communications** were very slow and the roads were terrible. The North, the West Country and Wales were difficult to govern because of their distance from the capital.
- Although most people were illiterate, **education was growing**. There were two universities in England (Oxford and Cambridge) and Elizabeth founded Trinity College in Dublin. A growing number of grammar schools were set up.
- The invention of the **printing press** aided the spread of new ideas and books became more affordable.

### Spain

- A newly unified nation, Spain was the **wealthiest and most powerful** European country in the sixteenth century.
- Its ruler during the Elizabethan period was Elizabeth's brother-in-law, **King Philip II**.
- Spain built a large **overseas empire** in Central and South America.
- It had close ties to the **Holy Roman Empire**.
- It **ruled over other territories**, including the Low Countries, parts of Italy and, from 1580, Portugal. It was strongly **Roman Catholic**.
- Spain had been a **traditional ally** of England but this changed and it became England's main enemy during Elizabeth's reign.

## Scotland

- **Ruled over by the Stuarts**. Although their royal family was closely related to the Tudors, Scotland was a traditional enemy of England, and the two countries had been at war many times.
- Henry VIII had spent huge amounts of money on an **invasion** of Scotland in the 1540s.
- Scotland's **main ally was France** (the Auld Alliance).
- The **Protestant Reformation** had spread there by the late 1550s.
- When Elizabeth became Queen, Scotland was ruled over by her young cousin, **Mary, Queen of Scots**.

## Ireland

- The **English King** had ruled as Lord of Ireland since the twelfth century. Henry VIII took more direct control in the 1540s, declaring himself to be the King of Ireland.
- In reality, the English only ruled a small area around Dublin known as **The Pale**, with local chieftains retaining a lot of power.
- Most Irish people were **Roman Catholic**, so Ireland could easily be used by the enemy as a base for attacking England.
- There were a number of **rebellions** here in the Tudor period.
- English Protestant settlers began to colonise Ireland in so-called 'PLANTATIONS'.

## The Netherlands

- Just across the English Channel, the Low Countries were ruled by the **Spanish Habsburgs**.
- Many **English merchants sold their goods here**. The cloth market at Antwerp was particularly important to England's economy.
- The **Protestant Reformation** spread here, as elsewhere in northern Europe, and there was a long period of rebellion against Spain in which England became involved.

## France

- A powerful country and **England's traditional enemy**. English monarchs historically claimed to be the rightful rulers of France, and the French intermittently paid a 'pension' – a kind of bribe – to England. Henry VIII went to war against France a number of times. The French had a strong alliance with Scotland.
- Although the **Roman Catholic** Church remained strong here, Protestant ideas spread.
- France was preoccupied with **religious wars** for much of Elizabeth's reign.

**ITALY**

## The Papacy

- **The Pope** was the head of the Roman Catholic Church. He lived in the Vatican in Rome.
- The Catholic Church was enormously **powerful and wealthy**, and it was also corrupt. People such as Martin Luther started to criticise the Catholic Church in the early part of the sixteenth century.
- This led to the **Reformation**. Those who protested became known as **Protestants**. The Church in Western Europe split, with many northern European countries becoming Protestant. England broke away from Rome in the 1530s under Henry VIII.

# Where did the Tudors come from?

In the fourteenth century, King Edward III and his dutiful Queen, Philippa of Hainault, had produced no less than five surviving sons. Although producing 'heirs and spares' has always been a marker of royal success, Edward and Philippa's marriage had been almost too fruitful for the good of England. The huge royal family descended into a power struggle between two branches, the House of Lancaster and the House of York. The Wars of the Roses, or the Cousins' War as it was called at the time, raged for 30 years, triggered by Henry VI's descent into madness in the 1450s. The final **Yorkist** king was Richard III. Richard has gone down in history as an evil man, allegedly involved in the murder of his two nephews, the Princes in the Tower, in order to gain the crown for himself.

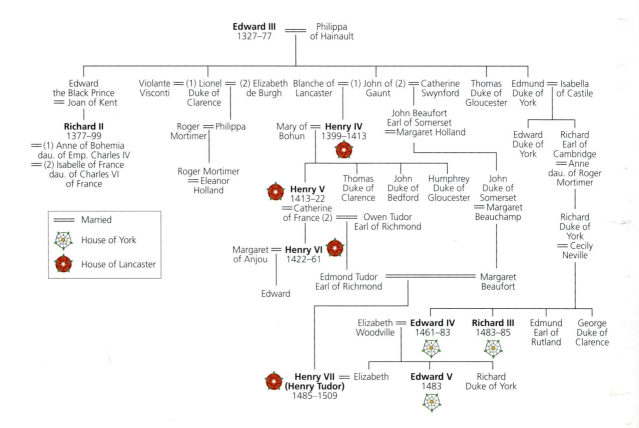

You can see from the family tree that Henry Tudor's claim to the throne was weak, but he was the only **Lancastrian** left standing. In August 1485 he landed in Wales and marched to meet Richard in battle at Bosworth Field. Richard was killed. This battle finally ended the long civil war.

Henry Tudor was crowned Henry VII and the Tudor DYNASTY was founded. Henry was mindful of the weakness of his situation and did all he could to shore up his position. He married Richard's niece, Elizabeth of York, to cement his control. This united the two warring families. This was symbolised through the red and white Tudor Rose.

Henry VII was unfairly regarded as a miser. Actually, he was a shrewd financial manager who avoided costly wars abroad and amassed great wealth at home, not really out of greed but as a means of maintaining his control. He negotiated brilliant alliances with both Spain and Scotland through marrying off his children. By the time of his death, although deeply unpopular, Henry VII left a secure and prosperous inheritance for his successors.

# Elizabeth and her government

**1**

In November 1558 church bells rang out in celebration of a new reign. England had a new Queen, named Elizabeth. She had been born 25 years earlier, the product of Henry VIII's notorious marriage to Anne Boleyn. Elizabeth inherited a weakened kingdom. England was in the grip of a deep and prolonged crisis. It had been ruled in succession by a paranoid tyrant, a delicate child and a fanatical HERETIC hunter. The economy was in ruins. The people had suffered repeated harvest failures and recurrent epidemics of disease. The timely ACCESSION of this young and beautiful woman was greeted with almost universal relief, but few at the time expected greatness of her. They would have been astounded to know that the accession date of 'Good Queen Bess' would be celebrated as a public holiday, Queen's Day, for hundreds of years to come. This chapter investigates how this happened.

# 1.1 Elizabeth's background and character

## FOCUS

Elizabeth I, the younger daughter of Henry VIII, was only the second QUEEN REGNANT to rule in England. She became Queen after the brief reign of her half-sister Mary Tudor. She inherited the throne at a very tricky time, yet maintained her authority for a reign that lasted almost 45 years. In topic 1.1 you will:

● examine Elizabeth's background and personality
● consider how far her character was shaped by her early experiences
● judge how well-prepared Elizabeth was for her role as Queen.

### FOCUS TASK A

#### Elizabeth's early life

As you read the next five pages draw up a simple timeline to summarise the main events in Elizabeth's life up to her accession in 1558. Include any dangers that she faced and events that affected her:

● relationship with her parents
● relationship with her siblings
● religion
● education.

You could illustrate it or turn it into a story strip.

## SOURCE 1

The family of Elizabeth I, painted in c.1545. Henry VIII is in the centre. His wife Jane Seymour is to the right of Henry and his son Edward is to the left, although in reality Jane actually died giving birth to Edward. Further to the left is Henry's elder daughter, Mary, and further to the right is his younger daughter, Elizabeth.

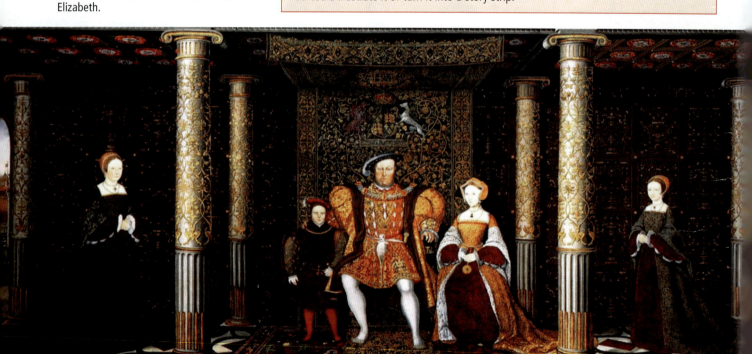

## Henry VIII's Great Matter

Henry VIII was married to his first wife, the Spanish princess Catherine of Aragon, for more than twenty years. Unfortunately, the marriage failed to produce a surviving male HEIR. A tragic series of miscarriages, stillbirths and infant deaths had left just one heir to the throne, a daughter, called Mary. The only historical precedent for this situation did not bode well. The last time England had had a

### THINK

1   Why do you think Henry VIII asked for his family to be painted as shown in Source 1 towards the end of his life?

female heir was in the twelfth century. This heir had been named Matilda, the daughter of Henry I. When her father died, her male cousin had taken the throne, triggering long and bloody civil war. At a time when the Tudor dynasty was still relatively new and with civil war within living memory – the Wars of the Roses had only ended in 1485 – Henry saw the situation as a disaster. He convinced himself that his marriage to Catherine was invalid and that God had punished the royal couple for their sin by denying them any surviving sons. Not only this, but Henry also become infatuated with another woman, an unconventional and manipulative lady at the Court named Anne Boleyn. Henry saw the young Anne as the solution to all of his problems, as he had every confidence that she could provide him with a son and heir.

Years and years of diplomatic pressure and bullying failed and the Pope refused to grant Henry the divorce he needed. When Anne fell pregnant, Henry took the drastic step of breaking with Rome and making himself the Supreme Head of the Church of England. This allowed Henry to free himself of his first wife and marry Anne Boleyn as his second. It was imperative that he married Anne before the birth of the child she was carrying so that it would be regarded as a legitimate heir to the throne. Much to Henry's anger, Anne gave birth to a girl. The baby was born on 7 September 1533 at the Palace of Greenwich and she was named Elizabeth in honour of her two grandmothers. In spite of the setback, an Act of Succession was nevertheless passed that confirmed the baby Elizabeth as the new heir to the throne. The law also declared Henry's elder daughter, Mary, to be ILLEGITIMATE.

## PROFILE

### Elizabeth's father: King Henry VIII

- Born June 1491, the younger son of Henry VII and Elizabeth of York, he became heir to the throne on the death of his older brother, Arthur, in 1502.
- Became King in 1509, aged seventeen. He was very popular, and regarded as handsome and intellectual when young.
- Married six times. His wives were Catherine of Aragon, Anne Boleyn, Jane Seymour, Anne of Cleves, Catherine Howard and Catherine Parr.
- Had three surviving legitimate children – the future Edward VI, Mary I and Elizabeth I.
- Broke from Rome in the early 1530s, setting up the Church of England, and dissolved the monasteries in the later 1530s.
- Had a reputation for laziness, often relying on the work of chief advisors, such as Wolsey and Cromwell.
- Went to war repeatedly against France and Scotland.
- Executed many of his close friends and relatives, such as Thomas More, Thomas Cromwell and Margaret Countess of Salisbury, for opposing him. As many as 72,000 people were executed in what has been referred to as a 'reign of terror'. By the end of his reign, he was a bloated, paranoid tyrant.
- Died January 1547, aged 55.

## PROFILE

### Elizabeth's mother: Anne Boleyn

- Born c.1501, the daughter of Sir Thomas Boleyn and Elizabeth Howard. Related to the English nobility.
- Lady in waiting at the COURT to Catherine of Aragon.
- Spent much of her youth in France.
- Very well educated, Anne had Lutheran (Protestant) sympathies.
- Began a liaison with Henry in the mid-1520s.
- Refused to become Henry's mistress, demanding to be his wife.
- Charismatic, ambitious, arrogant and manipulative.
- Became Henry's second wife. They were married for three years.
- Had one daughter, Elizabeth.
- Accused of adultery, TREASON and witchcraft.
- Executed May 1536.

# The King's daughter

Henry's marriage to Anne Boleyn quickly unravelled after the disappointment of the birth of another daughter. In May 1536, when Elizabeth was aged just two and a half, her mother was executed on trumped-up charges of treason, incest, adultery and witchcraft. Elizabeth herself would have no memory of her mother.

A Second Act of Succession declared Elizabeth, like her older half-sister, to be illegitimate with no right to inherit the throne. The birth of a male heir the following year to Henry and his third wife, Jane Seymour, seemed to relegate Elizabeth to a position of political irrelevance. As Henry VIII aged, his style of government became more tyrannical. In the late 1530s and early 1540s, many of Elizabeth's remaining Yorkist cousins were arrested and executed, as the paranoid King felt his position and that of the dynasty to be threatened. Exiled from Court, lonely and isolated from her family, Elizabeth rarely saw her father – meeting him only a few times throughout her life – but this distance only served to strengthen the immense love and admiration she appears to have felt towards him.

Although lacking a normal family life, Elizabeth was far from alone in these years. She lived with her own household in various royal residences in the country, the most significant being Hatfield in Hertfordshire. Initially, Elizabeth was taught by a governess, Kat Ashley, who became a lifelong friend. Later, despite being a woman, Elizabeth was given a brilliant education and was able to share some of the tutors employed to school her brother. The greatest intellectual influence on Elizabeth was undoubtedly her tutor, the Cambridge scholar Roger Ascham who replaced her previous tutor, William Grindal, when the latter died of plague. Ascham himself revelled in teaching such a conscientious and talented student as Elizabeth, and her love of learning gave her a reputation for seriousness. She was taught to use the modern italic style of handwriting, as favoured by Ascham, that had been developed in Italy during the RENAISSANCE. It contrasted sharply with the 'secretary hand' used by most people in England at the time, and it demonstrated how modern and advanced an education she had received. An accomplished linguist, by fourteen she could speak French, Italian, Spanish and Latin fluently, and was able to read Greek. Elizabeth was good at history and enjoyed writing poetry. Nor was Elizabeth just an intellectual. She was musical, athletic – being an accomplished horsewoman and dancer – and was skilled at needlework too.

During Elizabeth's teenage years, Henry's sixth wife, the Protestant reformer Catherine Parr, acted as a mother figure to Elizabeth. The two women got on well and Catherine influenced Elizabeth's Protestant religious views and the direction of her education. At this time, Elizabeth's position in the family did start to improve. She visited Court more often and lived for some of the time with her siblings. A Third Act of Succession, confirmed in 1544, had restored Elizabeth as an heir to the throne (although it did not technically make her legitimate), but stated that she could succeed only after her younger half-brother Edward and her older half-sister Mary. One or the other, or both, would be expected to produce children of their own. Therefore, while the arrangement raised Elizabeth's status, it also made it highly unlikely that she would ever become Queen.

## SOURCE 2

A portrait of the teenage Elizabeth (attributed to Guillaume Scrots).

## SOURCE 3

Extract from a letter by Roger Ascham, Elizabeth's tutor, in 1550.

*My illustrious mistress, the Lady Elizabeth, shines like a star. So much solidity of understanding, such courtesy and dignity, which I have never observed at so early an age. She hath the most ardent love of the true religion and the best kind of literature. Her mind is free from female weakness and she is endued [blessed] with a masculine power for hard work. No memory is more retentive than hers.*

## THINK

2   What impression does the painting in Source 2 give you of Elizabeth?
3   How might Elizabeth's education have affected her future ability as a Queen?

# The King's sister

In January 1547, Henry VIII died, to be succeeded by his nine-year-old son, Edward. Elizabeth reportedly wept uncontrollably when told of her father's death. Elizabeth had been fairly close to her brother Edward until this point, but once he became King, Edward VI quickly became aloof and arrogant. Like Elizabeth, he had been born after the break with Rome and was a staunch Protestant. Unlike Henry VIII, who had simply put himself in charge of the English Church but remained a Catholic at heart, Edward and his government brought about radical changes to actual religious practice and beliefs. Colourful images and stained glass windows were removed from churches, and the English language rather than Latin became widely used in sermons and prayer. How far the boy king really drove his government, or whether he was simply manipulated by his ministers, is a matter of debate, but either way Edward's reign was certainly tainted by political instability. Until the end of 1549, the power behind the throne was his uncle, his mother's brother, the Duke of Somerset. Following serious rebellions and having alienated many, including the King, through his arrogance, Somerset fell from power and was later executed on charges of treason.

It was Somerset's younger brother, Thomas Seymour, who embroiled Elizabeth in her first serious political crisis. He had married Elizabeth's step-mother, Catherine Parr – soon after Henry VIII's death – and Elizabeth lived in their household. An outrageous flirtation between Elizabeth and Seymour developed, which led to a grave scandal that had the potential to place Elizabeth's life in considerable danger. Seymour was accused of treason and executed in 1549. As part of the investigation, Elizabeth was questioned as it was suggested that Thomas Seymour was plotting to overthrow Edward and marry Elizabeth. Elizabeth managed to convince her investigators of her innocence in the matter and she escaped from the affair, embarrassed but nevertheless maintaining her freedom, status and, most importantly, her life. The episode, humiliating as it was for Elizabeth, probably taught her some invaluable political lessons about how to behave in future. She learned to keep her distance and to trust nobody.

Four years later, Elizabeth's young brother lay on his deathbed at just fifteen. Unmarried and childless, the dying boy was manipulated by his advisor the Duke of Northumberland into overriding the Third Act of Succession and Henry's will. Edward was persuaded to name his Protestant cousin Lady Jane Grey as his heir in place of his two half-sisters, and the Privy Council was bullied into accepting the change. Thus, when Edward died in the summer of 1553 it was Jane, not Mary, who was proclaimed Queen.

**PROFILE**

### Elizabeth's brother: Edward VI

- Born October 1537, the son of Henry VIII and his third wife Jane Seymour. His mother died within days of his birth.
- Became King aged only nine years old.
- The country was initially ruled by his uncle, the Duke of Somerset, as Lord Protector, until his fall from power and execution.
- The Duke of Northumberland later emerged as Somerset's replacement as Edward's chief minister.
- A strict Protestant who introduced an English prayer book and destroyed images in churches.
- Poverty grew as massive **INFLATION** was a problem throughout his reign.
- He faced serious rebellions in 1549 because of his changes to the Church and the country's economic problems.
- Declared Lady Jane Grey his heir on his deathbed.
- Died of tuberculosis in July 1553, aged fifteen.

## SOURCE 4

Extract from Henry VIII's will.

*As to the succession of the Crown, it shall go to Prince Edward and heirs of his body. In default to his daughter Mary and heir of her body, upon condition that she shall not marry without the written and sealed consent of the majority of the members of the Privy Council appointed by him to his son Prince Edward. In default to his daughter Elizabeth upon like condition. In default to the heirs of the body of Lady Frances, eldest daughter of his late sister the French Queen.*

**THINK**

4  Why was Henry's will (see Source 4) ignored when Edward died?

## The Queen's sister

Shortly after Lady Jane Grey, 'the Nine Days' Queen', was defeated, Mary and Elizabeth rode into London together triumphantly. This public show of unity disguised the deep gulf that divided the sisters. The accession of Mary, known ever since as 'Bloody Mary', made Elizabeth's position very difficult. A zealous Catholic, Mary was fiercely proud of her Spanish heritage. The new Queen passionately hated Elizabeth's mother Anne Boleyn for displacing her own mother as Queen, and she hated Elizabeth personally as the product of what she regarded as a bigamous marriage. She also hated Elizabeth's youth and beauty, and her Protestant faith. While Mary's regime rounded up Protestant heretics, burning nearly 300 of them over five years, Elizabeth outwardly conformed by attending the Catholic mass, but Mary viewed her sister with deep suspicion.

The situation was further complicated by the fact that, at 37 years old, Mary was as yet unmarried and childless, thus making Elizabeth her heir. Mary swiftly negotiated a marriage to her kinsman, Philip of Spain, provoking Wyatt's Rebellion in 1554. Outraged at what was seen as a Spanish takeover, thousands of rebels marched into London, but the rebellion quickly collapsed. Mary commanded Elizabeth to go to Whitehall Palace, where the Queen could keep an eye on her, but Elizabeth claimed she was ill and unable to make the journey. Elizabeth, suspected of working secretly with the rebels, faced a terrifying ordeal when Mary ordered her arrest and had her imprisoned in the Tower of London. Under torture, Wyatt claimed that he had written to Elizabeth and that she had approved of the rebellion, but he later retracted his statement about her involvement just before his execution. Imprisoned at the Tower for two horrendous months, Elizabeth wrote a long letter to her sister protesting her innocence. She was eventually released when no solid evidence against her could be found. Elizabeth was not free, however, and was kept under HOUSE ARREST firstly at Woodstock in Oxfordshire and later at her own palace of Hatfield.

## Accession

Elizabeth's tense relationship with Mary continued until Mary's death. Childless and having suffered two phantom pregnancies, borne out of her desperate desire to secure a Catholic succession, Mary gradually weakened in 1558. Then, on a single day, two deaths momentously changed the course of English history. Although she knew that the end was near, Mary had obstinately refused to officially proclaim Elizabeth her heir until just a few days before her death. The 42-year-old Queen finally died shortly after hearing mass at about 7 o'clock in the morning of 17 November, followed twelve hours later by her cousin and key Catholic advisor, Cardinal Reginald Pole. Messengers rode from St James' Palace to Hatfield, where Elizabeth was living. Legend has it that Elizabeth, found sitting underneath an oak tree in the park, was informed of her sister's death and her own accession by being handed the coronation ring. She is said to have proclaimed, 'This is the Lord's doing, and it is marvellous in our eyes!' Having consulted the advice of an astrologer, Dr John Dee, Elizabeth selected a date for her coronation. In a solemn and spectacular ceremony, Elizabeth was anointed with holy oil and crowned Queen in Westminster Abbey on 15 January 1559, beginning a reign of more than 40 years.

### PROFILE

#### Elizabeth's sister: Mary I

- Born February 1516, the daughter of Henry VIII and Catherine of Aragon.
- Parents' marriage annulled, making her illegitimate, in 1533.
- Restored to the succession in 1543.
- Became Queen July 1553, aged 37.
- Married her cousin, Philip of Spain. There were no children.
- Wyatt's Rebellion threatened her position in 1554.
- A strict Roman Catholic, she restored the authority of the Pope in England.
- Burned 282 Protestant heretics at the stake.
- Massive inflation, two harvest failures and epidemics of disease blighted the reign.
- England and Spain went to war against France, and England lost Calais, its last French possession, in 1558.
- Died November 1558, aged 42.

### THINK

5  What does Elizabeth's letter to her sister (see Source 5) suggest about her personality?

6  Why do you think Elizabeth's accession was welcomed by the English people?

### SOURCE 5

Elizabeth's protestation of innocence.

*I protest before God … that I never practised, counselled, nor consented to anything that might be prejudicial to your person anyway, or dangerous to the state by any means.*

This picture shows part of the letter written by Elizabeth to her sister Mary in March 1554 after Wyatt's Rebellion. You can see the lines she drew across the page so that nothing else could be added later.

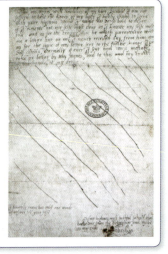

# Conclusion

Elizabeth's life before her accession was unhappy, dysfunctional and brimming with danger. Having lost her own mother as a toddler, and lacking a harmonious relationship with either her father or siblings, Elizabeth twice came dangerously close to execution for treason. However, unlike her sister Mary, whose traumatic life experiences left her embittered and emotionally damaged, Elizabeth's early life did the opposite. Elizabeth's miraculous survival served to strengthen her character and mould her into the cautious, clever and courageous Queen she became.

## SOURCE 7

Hatfield House in Hertfordshire where Elizabeth spent much of her childhood and early adult life.

## FOCUS TASK B

### Was Elizabeth ready to be queen?

You have been compiling a timeline of Elizabeth's life up to 1558.

1 Choose three events or developments that you think were particularly significant in shaping Elizabeth's character. Explain your choice.
2 Now imagine Elizabeth has to apply for the job of Queen. Use your findings to write her application. Remember she has to 'sell' herself as a good candidate for the role. Consider including:
- Her date of birth
- Family background
- Education
- Religion
- Personality and skills
- Key experiences
- Opinions regarding her predecessors
- Priorities and ideas for the future

## TOPIC SUMMARY

### Elizabeth's background and character

- The Tudors were a relatively new dynasty, having only come to power with Elizabeth's grandfather at the end of the Wars of the Roses in 1485.
- Elizabeth's father, Henry VIII, had broken with Rome in order to marry her mother Anne Boleyn.
- Elizabeth was declared illegitimate but was later restored to the succession in the 1540s.
- Elizabeth was highly intelligent and well educated, with firm Protestant views.
- Elizabeth had an awkward and dangerous position during the reigns of her siblings, facing two separate allegations of treason.
- Elizabeth succeeded her Catholic half-sister, Mary, in 1558 at a time of crisis in England.

## SOURCE 6

From *Elizabeth I* by W. MacCaffrey (1993).

*Elizabeth had undergone a useful apprenticeship in the art of politics, but the skills she learned were necessarily those derived from her own circumstances of extreme vulnerability. She had developed a strategy of caution, of immobility, of playing as few cards as possible, waiting and hoping on events. She was yet to learn the skills required for the exercise of rulership – making decisions, giving commands and ensuring those commands were obeyed … Elizabeth's experience was very limited.*

## THINK

7 According to MacCaffrey in Source 6, how well equipped was Elizabeth to be Queen?
8 How might a study of Hatfield House (Source 7) help you to understand Elizabeth's early life?

## PRACTICE QUESTION

Explain what was important about Elizabeth's experiences before she became Queen.

## TIP

Make sure you can remember several events from Elizabeth's childhood and early adulthood that had an effect on her personality. For each event make sure you can say *how* it affected her.

## KEYWORDS

Make sure you know what these words mean and are able to use them confidently in your own writing. See the glossary on page 94 for definitions.
- Accession
- Court
- Dynasty
- Heir
- Heretic
- Illegitimate
- Queen Regnant
- Renaissance
- Treason

# 1.2 Elizabethan politics

## FOCUS

Elizabeth inherited a political system that was faction ridden and inefficient. Her Court, Privy Council and Parliament were all based in London, and Elizabeth never even visited vast swathes of the country she ruled. Even so, she was a formidable monarch who managed to maintain her authority for nearly 45 years, skilfully utilising people and institutions to bolster her position. In topic 1.2 you will:

- examine the role of the Royal Court, Privy Council and Parliament under Elizabeth
- assess the roles played by Elizabeth's key ministers and understand how and why England faced a political decline by the 1590s
- judge how far Elizabeth maintained control as an effective ruler.

## THINK

1 Look at Source 1. Why do you think Elizabeth decided to go on progress so often during her reign?

## SOURCE 1

Elizabeth depicted on progress in c1600. She is shown with key members of her Court. Elizabeth was famous for her royal progresses, where she would travel around with her household and stay in various country houses, hosted by members of the nobility.

## FOCUS TASK A

### How did Elizabeth run her government?

Create a table like this:

| Feature | Explanation | How this helped Elizabeth (with examples) | What might go wrong (with examples) |
|---------|-------------|-------------------------------------------|-------------------------------------|
|         |             |                                           |                                     |

As you read pages 16–25 fill out rows for the following: Royal Court, progresses, patronage, Privy Council, Parliament.

# Elizabeth's problems at her accession

People question my ability to rule because I am a woman.

I want to turn the country's religious policy upside down again and re-establish Protestantism as the official religion.

I am unmarried and have no children.

I am young and inexperienced.

I need to decide who to appoint as my advisors.

We are at war with France and have no allies.

My people are living in poverty and liable to rebel.

People question my legitimacy and whether I should be Queen at all!

My government has inherited massive debts from my sister Mary.

## SOURCE 2

An extract from the diary of Sir Julius Caesar. Elizabeth stayed at his house for one night during a progress in 1590.

*The Queen visited my house in Mitcham and supped and lodged there, and dined the next day. I presented her with a gown of cloth of silver, richly embroidered; a black mantle [cloak] with pure gold; a hat of taffeta, white with several flowers; a jewel of gold set with rubies and diamonds. Her Majesty left my house after dinner with exceeding good contentment. This entertainment cost £700.*

## The Royal Court

The Royal Court was a mobile operation, not confined to a particular building. Run by the Lord Chamberlain, the Court was simply located wherever the Queen was. It consisted of the Queen's household, made up of about 500 nobles, advisors, officials and servants who all lived with her and competed for power and influence. They were called COURTIERS. In an age of PERSONAL MONARCHY, access to the Queen was crucial to any politician. The Court had been a centre of political power throughout the Tudor period. The economical Elizabeth, short of money, did not build any palaces herself, but did inherit and maintain a number of royal residences. Her favourite was Richmond, a comfortable residence built by her grandfather. In central London, the key residence was the sprawling Whitehall Palace that covered about twenty acres with its gardens, orchards, tennis courts and tiltyard used for tournaments. There was also St James' Palace, Hampton Court, Greenwich and Nonsuch, where she enjoyed hunting. As well as the luxurious palaces, the Tower of London and Windsor Castle served as secure places to be used in times of crisis. She disliked the Tower but adored Windsor and in fact Windsor Castle was the only residence where Elizabeth spent any money at all on alterations during her reign, having a terrace and gallery built there.

## Progresses

Most summers, Elizabeth would travel with her Court on tours called PROGRESSES, visiting the homes of the nobility. Her journeys covered the South East, Midlands and East Anglia. Historian Christopher Haigh has called them 'major public relations exercises', which allowed Elizabeth to be seen by her subjects regularly, to build up a relationship with her people and to flatter the nobles she chose to stay with. It would have been quite a sight to behold, as the Court crawled from house to house with up to 400 wagons piled high with clothes, linen, documents and furnishings, including the Queen's own bed, which she always travelled with. Wherever she went, she was given a magnificent welcome. To her subjects, she would appear as a goddess, parading in her finery. Progresses also served more practical purposes. They allowed the thrifty Elizabeth to live in luxury at the expense of her subjects, as the nobility all desperately tried to impress through their extravagance and generosity in providing the Queen and her courtiers with sumptuous accommodation, food and entertainment. The journeys also removed the Court from the sweltering capital at times when plague was rife and the absence of the household meant that the filthy Royal palaces could be fumigated before the Queen's return.

# Performance

The Court served a number of functions: as well as being a social hub, providing the Queen and her courtiers with a home and entertainment, it was a political nerve-centre. It also served to give an impression of power by displaying the Queen's magnificence to the nobility and visiting foreign guests through art and culture. There were lavish banquets, elaborate masques, musical performances, plays and tournaments that all acted as subtle PROPAGANDA, glorifying Elizabeth's image. Strict court ceremonies were followed that encouraged loyalty and obedience to Elizabeth. On feast days, the Queen dined in public with much pomp and ceremony, marching from the Chapel to Dining Hall behind her councillors who carried her SCEPTRES and sword of state. Such rituals followed strict rules and were well rehearsed and were designed to impress and magnify the mystique of monarchy. Elizabeth understood the importance of performance, playing the part to perfection.

## SOURCE 3

Elizabeth in her Privy Chamber.

# Patronage

In Henry VIII's time, the monarch's private apartments – the Privy Chamber – had been a crucial power hub, with the King's friends and personal attendants also being the key politicians. With a woman on the throne, the political nature of the Privy Chamber was reduced – as it was staffed by females. Elizabeth dealt with this situation by using a system of patronage. This involved showing favouritism by giving particular men important jobs. She managed this very carefully. She gave her male courtiers political roles and was equally careful to give key politicians places at Court. The jobs given were highly sought after, because they brought not only wealth but also prestige to the individual. Although it was a highly corrupt system, it was very effective. It caused intense competition and rivalries between people. This suited Elizabeth very well, because it made everybody totally loyal to her. It also ensured that the Court remained a political centre and made sure that Elizabeth remained at the heart of the whole political system.

## DEBATE

- Historians have traditionally praised Elizabeth for her skill and ability as a ruler, holding her personally responsible for the achievements of her reign.
- This is perhaps misleading and historians have to an extent been deceived by the propaganda produced during Elizabeth's reign.
- Not until the 1950s and 1960s was proper consideration given to the contributions made by Elizabeth's key ministers to the period's successes.

## THINK

4  How did the role of the Privy Chamber change under Elizabeth?

# The Privy Council

The Privy Council co-ordinated financial departments, law courts such as the Star Chamber, and regional bodies such as the Council of the North. It issued instructions to local officials such as Lord Lieutenants and Justices of the Peace. Members were generally from the nobility, GENTRY and the Church, but Elizabeth could choose and dismiss members of her Privy Council as she chose. Elizabeth delegated well and the workload of her Privy Council increased dramatically during her reign. The Privy Council met at Court almost daily, but Elizabeth did not always attend meetings. She came to trust her Privy Council, rarely interfering on a day-to-day basis. However, she kept accurate notes to monitor their work.

The key role of the Privy Council was to advise and direct policy but the Queen was not obliged to take their advice. In fact, Elizabeth often demonstrated her right to ignore their advice, making a strong statement about her own political independence. Ultimately it was Elizabeth who made policy decisions. Nevertheless, the Council had considerable powers. It could issue proclamations in the Queen's name, which had the force of law. It could command the arrest and imprisonment of individuals, although they rarely exercised such powers. The Council also proved skilful at guiding parliamentary business on behalf of the Queen.

# The structure of government under Elizabeth

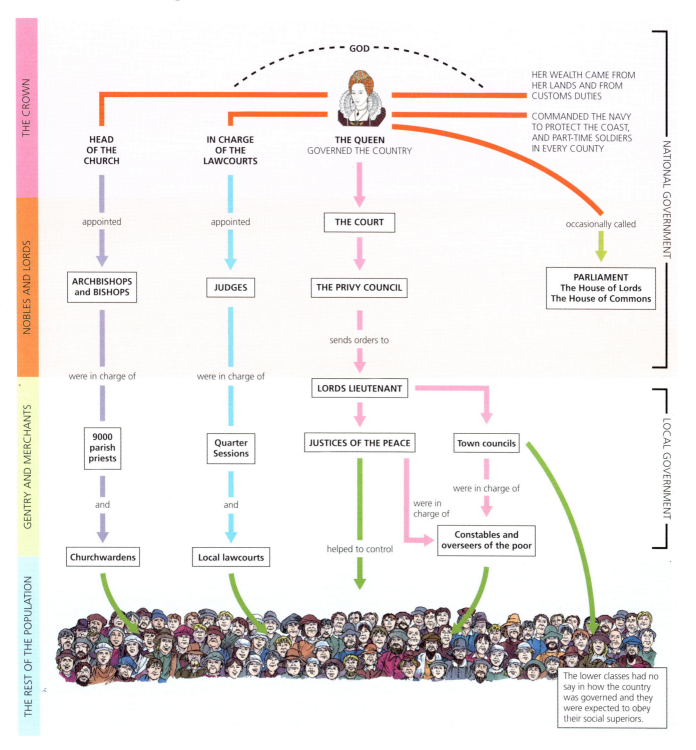

GOD

THE CROWN

HER WEALTH CAME FROM HER LANDS AND FROM CUSTOMS DUTIES

COMMANDED THE NAVY TO PROTECT THE COAST, AND PART-TIME SOLDIERS IN EVERY COUNTY

**HEAD OF THE CHURCH**

**IN CHARGE OF THE LAWCOURTS**

**THE QUEEN** GOVERNED THE COUNTRY

NATIONAL GOVERNMENT

NOBLES AND LORDS

appointed

appointed

THE COURT

occasionally called

ARCHBISHOPS and BISHOPS

JUDGES

THE PRIVY COUNCIL

PARLIAMENT The House of Lords The House of Commons

were in charge of

were in charge of

sends orders to

GENTRY AND MERCHANTS

LORDS LIEUTENANT

LOCAL GOVERNMENT

9000 parish priests

Quarter Sessions

JUSTICES OF THE PEACE

Town councils

were in charge of

and

and

were in charge of

Churchwardens

Local lawcourts

helped to control

Constables and overseers of the poor

THE REST OF THE POPULATION

The lower classes had no say in how the country was governed and they were expected to obey their social superiors.

SOURCE 4

**SOURCE 4**

Elizabeth's comments to Cecil when she appointed him to the Privy Council in November 1558.

*I have this judgement of you, that you will not be corrupted with any gift, you will be faithful to the state, and without respect of my private will, you will give me the best advice; if you know anything to be declared to me in secret, you will tell only me and I will keep it confidential.*

**SOURCE 5**

A.G.R. Smith on Cecil.

*His labour and care … were so incessant and his study so great as, in cases of necessity, he turned neither for meat, sleep or rest, till his business was brought to some end. This industry … caused all his friends to pity him and his very servants to admire him.*

**SOURCE 6**

From a report by the Spanish Ambassador.

*Her temper was so bad that no Councillor dared to mention business to her and when even Cecil did so, she told him that she had been strong enough to lift him out of the dirt, and she was able to cast him down again.*

**SOURCE 8**

Robert Naunton, a member of Elizabeth's Court, reminisces in the 1630s.

*She ruled much by factions and parties, which she made, upheld and weakened as her own great judgement advised.*

**THINK**

5 Read Sources 4–7. Why did Elizabeth choose Cecil as her chief advisor?

6 How convincing is Source 5's portrayal of Cecil?

7 Read Source 8. Why might Elizabeth have encouraged rivalries between her councillors?

8 Add notes to your Focus Task table about the Privy Council.

# Elizabeth's Privy Council

Three days after becoming Queen, Elizabeth said, 'I consider a multitude doth make rather disorder and confusion than good council'. What is more, Mary's Catholic Council could act as a barrier to re-establishing Protestantism. Elizabeth's first Privy Council was a clever compromise. By January 1559, she had appointed nineteen members (far more manageable and efficient than Mary's 40-member Council). Half were drawn from Mary's Council to maintain experience and avoid alienating important individuals. The other half were brand new, allowing Elizabeth to reward loyal followers and to promote men of ability. She was careful not to appoint any strong Catholics.

Over time Elizabeth increased in confidence. The nobility were gradually moved out and by the second half of her reign the Privy Council was a small, highly efficient group of educated, professional, full-time politicians, largely from the gentry. Some argue that this narrow membership became a weakness, causing resentment from powerful regional nobles and possibly encouraging rebellion.

By far the most important appointment Elizabeth made was one of her first – William Cecil. Elizabeth came to rely heavily on him. Their successful working relationship lasted until his death 40 years later. He was in continual contact with the Queen. All her correspondence passed through him. Cecil was loyal, but also knew how to manage the Queen. He threatened to resign to make her co-operate and carefully used Parliament to manipulate the Queen into taking the position he wanted. Elizabeth respected him for speaking his mind, but knew that he would carry out her wishes even if he personally disagreed. He also helped the Queen to manage the political patronage system and had his own patronage secretary – Sir Michael Hickes – who was responsible for dealing with the requests people made for various positions. Cecil had a difficult relationship with another key member of the Privy Council – the more radical and PURITAN Robert Dudley, a favourite of Elizabeth.

The key members of Elizabeth's council are shown opposite.

**SOURCE 7**

From a letter written by William Cecil to his son shortly before his death, summing up the nature of his relationship with Elizabeth.

*I do hold, and always will, this course in such matters as I differ in opinion from Her Majesty: as long as I may be allowed to give advice I will not change my opinion, but as a servant I will obey Her Majesty's commandment, presuming that she being God's chief minister here, it shall be God's will to have her commandments obeyed.*

# Divide and rule

The members of the Privy Council were ambitious, but Elizabeth was careful to control them. She sometimes showed affection and rewarded her ministers, but she could show displeasure too. She excluded both Dudley and Walsingham from Court at various points, imprisoned others and even went as far as executing two members of her Council, Norfolk and Essex, for treason. Elizabeth also deliberately appointed men who were hostile towards each other. By forcing rival factions to work together on the Council, Elizabeth played a game of 'divide and rule', which meant the men would compete with each other for her affection. They would give her contrasting advice, which would then allow her to make measured decisions. Whichever course of action she pursued, she could be sure she would have some support. Nevertheless, in spite of their differences – on religion, foreign policy issues and the Queen's marriage – the group established by Elizabeth maintained a professional working relationship and ran the country effectively and efficiently for much of her reign.

### Sir William Cecil, Lord Burghley

- Born 1520. A member of the Lincolnshire gentry.
- Moderate Protestant who had studied law at Cambridge.
- Enormously intelligent and very hard working.
- Past experience as a Member of Parliament and a member of Edward VI's Council.
- Made Secretary of State in November 1558.
- A stabiliser. Like Elizabeth, he wanted to avoid war and unite the nation through moderate policies. He was naturally conservative, and like the Queen disliked being rushed into rash decisions.
- Elizabeth admired the fact that Cecil spoke his mind if he disagreed with her or other councillors.
- Elizabeth relied heavily on Cecil, counting on his loyalty and trusting him completely.
- Given the title Lord Burghley in 1571 and made Lord Treasurer the following year.
- Regularly attended the House of Commons and, later, the House of Lords. A very skilful parliamentary manager.
- Died 1598, replaced as Elizabeth's chief minister by his son, Robert.

### Robert Dudley, Earl of Leicester

- Born 1533. Younger son of the disgraced Duke of Northumberland who had been executed at the beginning of Bloody Mary's reign.
- Like Elizabeth, he spent some of Mary's reign locked in the Tower of London.
- A childhood friend and favourite of Elizabeth, he was good looking and there were many rumours of a romance between Dudley and Elizabeth.
- A member of the Court, he was made Master of the Horse, making him personally responsible for Elizabeth's safety.
- Highly ambitious, he became a PRIVY COUNCILLOR in 1562, proving to be a conscientious worker.
- A radical and a Puritan, he frequently argued with Cecil about the succession, religion and foreign policy.
- Given the title Earl of Leicester in 1564.
- Died 1588.

### Sir Francis Walsingham

- Born 1532. From Norfolk gentry
- Attended Cambridge University and studied law.
- Fervent Puritan. Had fled into exile in Mary Tudor's reign and studied at Padua University in Italy.
- Fiercely loyal to Elizabeth.
- Entered Parliament as an MP in 1558.
- His ability at languages and foreign contacts made him useful to Elizabeth and he started working with the government in 1568. Served as AMBASSADOR in Paris in the early 1570s.
- Appointed to the Privy Council in 1573, became Secretary of State with special responsibility for foreign affairs. Knighted in 1577.
- Could be blunt. Frequently clashed with Cecil. An ally of Dudley.
- A superb organiser. Was in charge of the Elizabethan 'secret service'. He was a highly efficient 'spy master', controlling a network of informers at home and abroad, and uncovering numerous plots against Elizabeth.
- Died 1590.

### Sir Christopher Hatton

- Born 1540. From the Northamptonshire gentry.
- Studied law at Oxford University.
- Elizabeth was impressed by his dancing at Court and promoted him. He became a Gentleman of the Privy Chamber and the Captain of the Queen's Bodyguard.
- Loyal, kind, clever and hardworking. Helped organise Elizabeth's famous progresses.
- A moderate Protestant, he hated Puritans and sympathised with Catholics.
- Elected to parliament several times. Helped Elizabeth control the MPs and secure their support.
- Became Lord Chancellor in 1587, in charge of judges and law Courts.
- Died 1591.

**THINK**

9 Study the four profiles carefully. What were the key similarities and differences between Elizabeth's key ministers? Consider their background, religion and personality.

# The role of Parliament

The monarch decided when Parliament should meet and for how long. Parliament was called if the monarch needed new laws to be passed or wanted to introduce new taxes.

Elizabeth regarded Parliament as an inconvenient necessity. Continuing in the tradition of her father, her very first Parliament in 1559 created a new Protestant church by restoring the royal supremacy over the Church of England. This undid Mary's short-lived attempt at a Catholic restoration. Since Elizabeth's father Henry VIII had secured the break from Rome in the 1530s through laws passed by Parliament, Parliament's importance had increased significantly. The idea had developed that the English monarch shared their power with Parliament in a kind of political partnership. However, it was not Parliament's role to govern, but simply to turn the policies of Elizabeth and her ministers into laws.

Elizabeth's financial problems meant that she had to rely heavily on parliamentary subsidies (taxes), which were asked for in all but two of the thirteen sessions of the reign. On almost all occasions, Elizabeth received what she asked for.

The main business enacted by each of Elizabeth's Parliaments is shown in the table below.

| Date | Main business enacted by Parliament |
| --- | --- |
| 1559 | Restoration of the royal supremacy over a Protestant Church of England. |
| 1563 | Approval of taxes to fund wars against France and Scotland. |
| 1566 | Taxes agreed to pay for an army sent to France. |
| 1571 | Taxes agreed to help defeat a rebellion in the North. Laws against the Pope and TRAITORS. |
| 1572 | MPs met to discuss the Queen's safety after discovery of a Catholic plot. |
| 1576 | MPs agreed to taxes even though the country was at peace. |
| 1581 | Taxes approved to pay for an army sent to Ireland. Anti-Catholic laws also passed. |
| 1584–85 | Laws against Catholic priests passed. More taxes granted. |
| 1586–87 | MPs granted taxes for war against Spain. |
| 1589 | MPs approved taxes to pay the costs of defeating the Spanish Armada the year before. |
| 1593 | Taxes granted for war against Spain and more anti-Catholic laws passed. |
| 1597–98 | More taxes granted and laws passed regarding the poor. |
| 1601 | Taxes granted to pay for war against Spain and to pay for the army in Ireland. |

## FACTFILE

### Parliament in the reign of Elizabeth

- Parliament was made up of two constituent parts: the House of Lords and the House of Commons.
- The House of Lords was the upper house and was more powerful, containing 90 PEERS. It was made up of members of the nobility and bishops. As Elizabeth created so few new lords, by the end of her reign there were just 55 members of the House of Lords and it was very much under her control.
- The House of Commons contained around 450 elected MPs. They were educated gentry, lawyers and merchants, and became more powerful during Elizabeth's reign. Two knights from each county and two BURGESSES from each borough attended.
- There were no formal political parties as exist today.
- England was not a democracy. Only landowners and wealthy citizens could vote for MPs, and these were a tiny minority of the population. In reality, MPs were usually nominated by either the crown or by a prominent nobleman rather than elected. The majority – the lower classes and all women – could not vote.
- A bill is a draft of a proposed law. For a bill to become law, it has to be passed as an Act of Parliament, meaning that both the House of Commons and the House of Lords had to approve of it.
- Before a bill was passed as an Act, a bill would be read three times in Parliament: the first reading would tell the members about the contents of the bill, the second reading would bring about debate after which it would be amended, and the third reading would be a final checking process before voting took place.
- Elizabeth possessed a royal veto, meaning she had the right to reject an Act of Parliament.
- Statistics on Parliament in the Elizabethan period:
  - Number of sessions: 13
  - Total number of weeks in session over 45 years: 140
  - Average number of weeks it met per year: 3
  - Number of years it did not meet: 29
  - Percentage of MPs who spoke in debates: 10 per cent
  - Average percentage of MPs who voted: 47 per cent
  - Total number of Acts passed: 434

## THINK

10 Study the table of business enacted by Parliament. What are the most common reasons Parliament met?

11 What do the statistics in the final point of the Factfile suggest about the importance of Parliament during Elizabeth's reign?

## SOURCE 9

A seventeenth-century drawing of Elizabeth I opening Parliament.

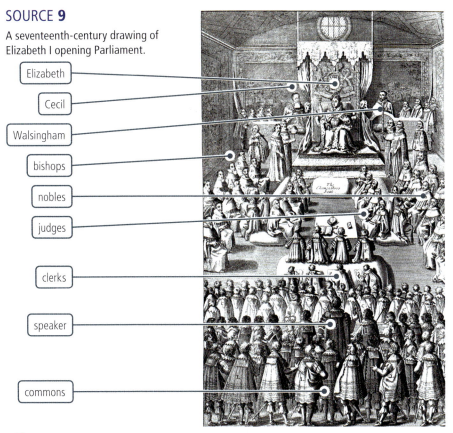

Elizabeth
Cecil
Walsingham
bishops
nobles
judges
clerks
speaker
commons

## Changes

Despite Elizabeth's attitude to Parliament during her reign, MPs became more self-confident in arguing against the Queen. This may have been because they were better-educated than in the past, with over half of them having had a university education. Members of Parliament were supposed to have special privileges, allowing them freedom of speech and freedom from arrest. Some heated debates did take place. MPs made complaints about issues that were not on the government agenda, such as Elizabeth's marital status, trading MONOPOLIES and religious grievances. Puritans, in particular, repeatedly used the House of Commons to organise and voice their opposition to the Queen's policies. Some have suggested that in this way, Elizabeth lost control during her reign.

However, Elizabeth made use of her powers to limit the influence of Parliament. As with her Council, she used the force of her own personality, attending Parliament in person when necessary and using speeches to both charm and bully its members. Additionally, she had the right to appoint the Speaker, who was able to control which topics were discussed and steer the direction of the debate. Furthermore, the Queen had the right to block measures proposed by MPs through using the royal veto. Elizabeth imposed limits on MPs' right to speak freely and did not shy away from imprisoning awkward MPs, such as Peter Wentworth who was imprisoned in 1576 for arguing for freedom of speech. Of course, Elizabeth was also able to dissolve any troublesome Parliament whenever she wished.

In addition to the Queen's direct influence, members of the Privy Council sat in both the House of Commons and House of Lords, providing a way for the government to control and manipulate parliamentary affairs. In reality, MPs were carefully considered by the Council before they were selected and local officials carefully supervised the elections when they took place. As so many MPs owed their seats to the patronage of the Queen or her councillors, their behaviour and independence was severely restricted.

## SOURCE 10

From *Elizabeth I* by Christopher Haigh (1988).

*Elizabeth adopted a tone of condescending superiority towards her Parliaments, confident that if she explained things often enough and slowly enough, the little boys would understand. For Elizabeth, parliamentarians were little boys – sometimes unruly and usually a nuisance, and always a waste of an intelligent woman's time. Queen Elizabeth did not like Parliaments and it showed.*

## SOURCE 11

Part of Elizabeth's 'Golden speech', delivered to the House of Commons in November 1601.

*I have reigned with your loves. I do not so much rejoice that God hath made me to be a Queen, as to be a Queen over so thankful a people. It is not my desire to live or reign longer than my life and reign shall be for your good. And though you have had many mightier and wiser princes sitting in this seat, you have never had, nor ever shall have, any that will love you better than I do.*

## SOURCE 12

From *Elizabeth I*, by Christopher Haigh (1988).

*Elizabeth's councillors nominated MPs, planned business in advance and tried to manage proceedings. Parliament was a most useful means of applying pressure on the Queen to accept policies she disliked – such as over marriage and the succession in 1563 and 1566, over religious reform in 1571, over anti-Catholic laws in 1581 and over the execution of Mary, Queen of Scots, in 1586.*

### THINK

12 Read Source 10. Why did Elizabeth attend Parliament and make speeches there if she had such a low opinion of its members?

13 According to Sources 10–12, who seems to have held real power in Elizabethan England: the Queen, her councillors, or Parliament?

14 Add notes about Parliament to your Focus Task table.

## DEBATE

- J.E. Neale argued in the 1930s and 1940s that Parliament's power grew in Elizabeth's reign.
- He suggested that MPs in the House of Commons deliberately planned confrontations with the Queen. They became more confident and independent, and Elizabeth lost control.
- Neale argued that the roots of the English Civil War in the 1640s lay in Elizabeth's reign.
- Later historians, such as G.R. Elton, disagree with Neale, emphasising co-operation rather than conflict between Elizabeth and Parliament.

### SOURCE 13

From *Elizabeth I* by Christopher Haigh (1988).

*In the new and bitter world of the 1590s, Elizabeth was shown to be politically bankrupt. The only answer she and those close to her could provide seemed to be 'more of the same'. Elizabeth lived up to her motto,* semper eadem, *always the same. She was a ruler overtaken by events.*

### SOURCE 14

*Tudor England* by John Guy (1988) explains Essex's motives for rebellion.

*When Elizabeth refused to renew [Essex's] patent of sweet wines … his credit structure collapsed. She had effectively condemned him to a life of poverty … Yet Essex's motivation went beyond this. A faction leader who was denied access to a monarch was an untenable position … After his disgrace, his urge to oust the Cecilian 'upstarts' … became obsessional.*

### THINK

15 In Source 13, what does Haigh suggest about the quality of Elizabeth's government by the end of her reign?

16 Read Source 14. Why did Essex decide to rebel in 1601?

# Years of decline

By the 1590s, Elizabeth's government was in crisis. The country had been seriously damaged by war, plague, increased poverty and repeated harvest failures. The patronage system that had worked so well started to break down, as a series of personal tragedies befell the Queen. One by one, her trusted councillors and contemporaries died: Dudley in 1588, Walsingham in 1590 and Hatton in 1591. So bereft was she when Dudley died, that she locked herself away in her room for days and Cecil had to order for the door to be broken down. Finally, in the greatest blow of all, Cecil himself died in August 1598. Elizabeth had come to rely heavily on these men. With their deaths she became increasingly angry, depressed and bad tempered, losing popularity and facing sharp criticism. People started to sense that she had reigned too long and that she stood in the way of much needed reform. Elizabeth had always had confidence in the personal devotion of her councillors and the most obvious and serious sign of Elizabeth losing her grip came in 1601, when the ageing Queen faced a rebellion organised by one of her favourites.

## Essex's Rebellion 1601

Just as rivalry between different groups had existed and been encouraged at the beginning of her reign, so too did it exist at the end. This had worked well in the past, with William Cecil and Dudley balancing each other out. As Elizabeth's 'old guard' disappeared, a new generation of ambitious politicians emerged that caused unrest in the Court and Council. The two main rivals in the Privy Council were Lord Burghley's son, Robert Cecil, and Dudley's step-son, the Earl of Essex. Robert Cecil had been a sickly child but he studied hard and was appointed to the Privy Council in 1591. He took on an increasingly heavy workload as his father aged and was made Secretary of State. He came to hold much power, having been trained by his father and by Walsingham in the art of spycraft. Cecil's rise to power angered the jealous Essex and the division in the Council became unhelpful. While Cecil was a shrewd and subtle political operator, Essex was a dashing young courtier who had caught Elizabeth's eye. However, he was unpredictable, and his actions often angered the Queen. He had annoyed the Queen by secretly marrying without her permission and when she later refused to promote one of his supporters, he actually lost his temper and insulted the Queen by shouting 'her conditions are as crooked as her carcass!' and turning his back on her in anger. Elizabeth then punched Essex, who almost drew his sword but instead stormed out of the meeting. After this, he was banished from Court.

Later, Essex was given yet another chance to redeem himself, when Elizabeth asked him to defeat a rebellion in Ireland being led by the Earl of Tyrone in 1598. Again, Essex miscalculated, making peace with Tyrone against Elizabeth's orders. While Essex was away fighting, the Queen promoted Cecil. Sparked by jealousy, on his return to Court, Essex burst into the Queen's bedchamber before she was wigged and gowned. For Elizabeth, this level of disrespect was the final straw. He was ordered before the Privy Council, and had to stand for five hours while he was interrogated. Later, charges were made which he had to listen to on his knees. He was again banned from Court and placed under house arrest. Losing all his jobs and his monopoly on sweet wines, his career was totally ruined.

Incensed by his fall, in early 1601 Essex gathered around 300 supporters, made up of a few unsuccessful courtiers and disgruntled unemployed soldiers. He began to fortify his mansion, Essex House, on The Strand. Rumours of treason and rebellion began to spread and Essex refused Elizabeth's demands for him to appear in front of the Privy Council. When four Privy Councillors went to his house to question him, he locked them up as hostages, and proceeded to march with his men to the centre of London in an effort to capture the Queen.

He underestimated Elizabeth and her government, and overestimated his own strength. The government responded decisively. Londoners were unimpressed and most of his supporters quickly deserted him when they were offered a pardon. Essex found his route blocked so he returned home, where his house was surrounded by Elizabeth's forces, giving him no choice but to surrender. The rebellion had lasted a mere twelve hours. Accused of being a traitor, Essex was executed at the Tower of London on 25 February 1601 – a swift and spectacular fall from grace for a former royal favourite, but also a sure sign of Elizabeth's fading powers.

## FOCUS TASK B

### Elizabeth's advice

You have been compiling a table showing how Elizabeth ran her government.

1 Where would you put Elizabeth on a scale of 1–5 if 1 was 'totally in control' and 5 was 'only a figurehead'? Write a paragraph to explain your reasons using examples from your table.

2 Now use your findings to write an instruction manual for Elizabeth's successor, giving practical advice about how to run the government effectively as a monarch in England, and using real examples from her reign.

Make sure you cover:

- The role of the monarch
- The importance of the Royal Court
- The work of the Privy Council
- The importance of individuals
- The role of Parliament
- Whether Elizabeth made any mistakes that her successors should avoid

## PRACTICE QUESTIONS

1 Explain what was important about the Privy Council in Elizabeth's reign.

2 Write an account of the ways in which a system of political patronage helped Elizabeth to govern England.

3 Write an account of the ways in which the Earl of Essex affected Elizabethan England.

## TOPIC SUMMARY

### Elizabethan politics

- Elizabeth was inexperienced when she became Queen, but she quickly became an expert politician.
- The Royal Court was a political centre with a corrupt patronage system and where different groups competed for power and influence.
- The Royal Court was also a social and cultural centre, designed to impress visitors with its magnificence and ceremony.
- The Queen famously went on progress most summers as public relations exercises.
- Elizabeth relied on a small group of trusted advisors who sat on a committee called the Privy Council.
- Elizabeth disliked Parliament, which was mainly called in order to grant taxes.
- Parliament grew in confidence and independence, at times being quite outspoken in its criticism of Elizabeth's government.
- Elizabeth's key advisors died, leaving her isolated and bitter towards the end of her life.
- A rebellion was mounted by one of her former favourites towards the end of her reign.

## PROFILE

### Robert Devereux, Earl of Essex

- Born in 1565, the son of Elizabeth's cousin, Lettice Knollys, and step-son of her old favourite, Robert Dudley, Earl of Leicester.
- Studied at Cambridge University.
- Young, eloquent and good-looking, he was a favourite with Elizabeth and popular with the people.
- He was also ambitious, arrogant and short-tempered.
- A military hero, he was an experienced soldier who fought in the Netherlands, France and Spain.
- Knowledgeable about foreign affairs, he joined the Privy Council in 1593.
- Married Walsingham's daughter.
- Disrespectful to Elizabeth on a number of occasions. They repeatedly had heated arguments although she always forgave him.
- Hated the Cecils.
- Eventually, he led a rebellion and was executed for treason in 1601.

## TIP

Make sure you can identify various people who helped Elizabeth to run her government and explain the contribution that they made.

## KEYWORDS

Make sure you know what these words mean and are able to use them confidently in your own writing. See the glossary on page 94 for definitions.

- Ambassador
- Courtiers
- Gentry
- Monopolies
- Patronage
- Peers
- Privy Councillors
- Progresses
- Propaganda
- Puritan
- Traitor

# 1.3 The succession crisis

**THINK**

1  How do you think a female monarch could make her gender an advantage rather than a disadvantage in a male-dominated society?

**FOCUS**

As a woman, Elizabeth faced considerable prejudice when she came to the throne. She was repeatedly pressurised to marry, but never did so and did not produce an heir, meaning that when she died, so too did the Tudor dynasty. In topic 1.3 you will:

● explore the problems facing female rulers in the sixteenth century
● consider the strengths and weaknesses of Elizabeth's various SUITORS and judge why she decided to remain unmarried
● examine the succession crisis Elizabeth faced during her reign and understand how this was resolved.

**SOURCE 1**

Elizabeth I shown dancing with her favourite, Robert Dudley, the Earl of Leicester.

**FOCUS TASK A**

**The succession crisis**

As you read pages 26–30 make notes under the following headings:

● **Attitudes:** how did Elizabeth's contemporaries view women and female rulers

● **Pressures:** how and why Elizabeth's ministers and Parliament pressurised her to marry when younger

● **Suitors:** the pros and cons of her various suitors

● **Heirs:** the potential successors to the throne on Elizabeth's death

**SOURCE 2**

David Starkey in *Elizabeth* (Episode 2, 2000, Channel 4).

*It is 1559. England has a newly crowned Queen. Elizabeth has overcome extraordinary obstacles to gain the crown, but her struggle isn't over. There's one thing about her that will lead to scandal, that will compromise her power, threaten her security and demand terrible personal sacrifice: that she is a woman.*

## Problems facing female rulers

Such was the prejudice against female rulers that Elizabeth's father had gone to enormous trouble to prevent a female succeeding to the throne. In his attempts to have a male heir he had broken from Rome and married six times. Despite his efforts Elizabeth's sister Mary had been the first Queen Regnant of England, proving that it could be done, but Mary's reign did not inspire confidence in the arrangement. Mary had taken a husband within a year of her accession, which had put England's political independence at risk. Mary died enormously unpopular after just a brief reign. Although people welcomed the accession of a beautiful young woman and a Protestant, it was more out of relief that Mary's regime had ended than out of joy that Elizabeth's had begun.

# A man's world

In such a man's world, few really thought that Elizabeth was up to the task of government. Women, it was feared, were weak and not suited intellectually or temperamentally to reign. Monarchs were thought to need traditionally masculine characteristics: physical strength, assertiveness and decisiveness. Queens were meant to be merely the wives of kings. They were supposed to be kind, religious and maternal. They were not supposed to rule. It was feared that chaos could be the result. A weak monarch and powerful nobles had led to the Wars of the Roses that had torn England apart just a century before. With a female monarch, the careful balance of groups at Court might be upset and many doubted the ability of a woman to control her male subjects. Moreover, a monarch had a duty to keep their country safe and to further its interests abroad, but Elizabeth could not be expected to lead her army into battle as a king might do.

However, there were examples of women ruling effectively at this time. Isabella of Castile had ruled Spain with distinction, and Marie de Guise had ruled Scotland with an iron fist as REGENT for her daughter. As Elizabeth got older, she came to see her gender not as a disadvantage but as a useful political weapon. It allowed her to charm and manipulate, to avoid situations she disliked and decisions she did not want to make. It also helped her create a powerful CULT of personality.

Elizabeth's pride was hurt by one piece of writing in particular. In the year of her accession, the Scottish Protestant John Knox wrote a book attacking female rulers, entitled *The First Blast of the Monstrous Trumpet Against Women*. Although Knox had been motivated to write by Bloody Mary and Marie de Guise, the timing was awful. Elizabeth succeeded in the same year as the book's release. She found the work insulting, and identified Knox as a political enemy rather than, as he could have been, a religious ally.

## SOURCE 3

From *The First Blast of the Trumpet Against the Monstrous Regiment of Women* by John Knox (1558).

*To promote a woman to bear rule, superiority, dominion, or empire above any realm, nation, or city, is repugnant to nature, an insult to God, a thing most contrary to his revealed will and approved ordinance, and finally, it is the subversion of good order, of all equity and justice… God, by the order of his creation, deprived women of authority and dominion… For who can deny but it is repugnant to nature, that the blind shall be appointed to lead those who can see? That the weak, the sick, and impotent persons shall nourish and keep the whole and strong? And finally, that the foolish, mad, and frenetic shall govern the discreet, and give counsel to such as be sober of mind? And such be all women, compared unto man, in bearing of authority. For their sight is but blindness; their strength, weakness; their counsel, foolishness; and their judgment, frenzy.*

# The marriage question

Elizabeth was 25 years old when she succeeded. By Tudor standards this was old to still be unmarried. She had not married because of her awkward position during her father's and siblings' reigns. Everybody assumed that marriage would be high on Elizabeth's list of priorities when she became Queen. They expected a suitable wedding to be quickly arranged. To add to the urgency, she was the last of Henry VIII's children. If she died without an heir, the Tudor dynasty would die too.

But Elizabeth hesitated and for years she kept people at home and abroad guessing as to whom she would choose and whether she would marry at all. Her Privy Council became annoyed, repeatedly pressing her to marry to solve the issue of the succession. Her Parliaments, encouraged by the Council, also tried to pressure her to marry. She gave vague answers and then famously lost her temper with her third Parliament in 1566 for daring to raise the issue. After this, Parliament was not allowed to discuss her marriage ever again.

## SOURCE 4

Thomas Becon, a Norfolk clergyman, in 1554.

*Thou hast set to rule over us a woman, whom nature hath formed to be in subjection to man… Ah, Lord, to take away the empire from a man and give it to a woman seemeth to be an evident token of thine anger towards us Englishmen.*

## SOURCE 5

Part of a speech Elizabeth made at Tilbury during the Spanish Armada.

*I know I have the body of a weak, feeble woman; but I have the heart and stomach of a king, and of a king of England, too.*

## SOURCE 6

William Cecil, speaking in 1566.

*Pray God would send our mistress a husband, and by time a son, that we may hope our posterity shall have a masculine succession.*

## SOURCE 7

Elizabeth's response to Parliament pressurising her to marry in 1566.

*I will never be by violence constrained to do anything. It is monstrous that the feet should direct the head! They are too feeble minded to discuss the issue.*

## SOURCE 8

L.J. Taylor-Smith (1984).

*Elizabeth came to value and adopt the masculine qualities of dominance, aggression and fearlessness, which made it impossible for her to assume the subservient role expected of a wife.*

## THINK

2 Why did the Council and Parliament pressurise Elizabeth to marry?

3 How convincing do you find Source 8 about Elizabeth's decision not to marry?

4 Make notes under headings 1 and 2 of the Focus Task about attitudes and marriage pressure.

# Marriage pros and cons

Having a husband would limit my personal freedom.

I would have to share my power with my husband.

Most of the suitable candidates for my hand are Catholic, but I am Protestant.

A foreign marriage would make a powerful alliance.

A foreign marriage might make enemies of other countries who feel rejected.

My sister Mary's marriage had caused rebellion.

Taking an English husband will unbalance the different groups at Court and cause problems.

I need to provide an heir to the throne to carry on the Tudor line.

My father's marriages worked out badly. He killed two of his wives, including my own mother.

### THINK

5    Study the marriage pros and cons above. Why did Elizabeth choose not to marry if she had so many options available?

### SOURCE 9

Elizabeth's reaction to Robert Dudley's attempt to give orders to her servants.

*I will have here but one mistress and no master!*

# Foreign suitors

Elizabeth received two early proposals: from Prince Eric of Sweden and from King Philip of Spain. She negotiated with the Swedes for years, but turned down Philip immediately. He was the widower of Elizabeth's sister Mary. He was keen to regain his title of King of England. He was Catholic, but his family were England's traditional allies against France. However, Elizabeth knew how badly he had treated her sister during their brief marriage. Nor did she forget that Mary's choice of Spanish husband had been so unpopular with the English people that it had caused rebellion. Their marriage had proved disastrous, providing no children and involving England in costly foreign wars that led to the loss of Calais, England's last French possession. She never seriously considered him, and he was insulted by the rejection.

Other foreign candidates included the son of the Holy Roman Emperor, Charles of Austria. He was also Catholic, but negotiations dragged on until 1567, when they eventually failed because Charles seemed unwilling to live in England.

# English suitors

Elizabeth was also not short of English suitors. Early in her reign, both the Earl of Arundel and Sir William Pickering hoped to marry Elizabeth. By far the most serious contender was her childhood friend and favourite, Robert Dudley, the Earl of Leicester. The two were close friends. Many historians agree that Elizabeth genuinely loved him. Within two years of her becoming Queen there was strong belief at Court that Elizabeth had decided to marry him.

He desperately wanted to marry her but unfortunately was already married. When his wife, Amy, died in mysterious circumstances – her lifeless body was found at the foot of a staircase – all hopes of a marriage between Dudley and the Queen, ironically, were dashed. An inquest was held. Amy's death was ruled accidental, but it all seemed a little too convenient for the love-struck Queen and ambitious courtier. The rumours that Amy Dudley had possibly been murdered – either by Dudley or on Elizabeth's orders – meant a marriage between the two would have been scandalous. It was out of the question. Dudley waited for years for the Queen to change her mind, and only got married – much to her fury – in 1578, to her cousin, the Countess of Essex.

# The last suitor

As Elizabeth aged, the endless rounds of marriage negotiations continued. By the late 1570s, attention focused on the Duke of Alençon, a younger brother of the King of France. Although over twenty years younger than Elizabeth, physically deformed and a Catholic, he seemed a serious prospect and the two appeared to be genuinely fond of each other. Elizabeth affectionately called him her 'frog'. The Privy Council were bitterly divided on the match: Cecil was in favour but Walsingham and Dudley were opposed. However, after the St Batholomew's Day Massacre in 1572, when thousands of Protestants were murdered, the French were very unpopular in England. Propaganda pamphlets were published against the Queen marrying Alençon. So, despite considerable opposition from the Council, the Queen called off the negotiations, and wrote a poem 'On Monsieur's Departure' which seems to show genuine regret at his loss.

Despite considering so many suitors, it is unclear whether Elizabeth ever truly wanted to marry any of them. It could be that she simply played out the negotiations as a diplomatic game. Whether she remained single by deliberate design or by historical accident is still debated.

Alençon was the last suitor seriously considered by Elizabeth, and by the time Elizabeth entered her 50s her cult status as the 'Virgin Queen' who was married to England became firmly established.

# Possible heirs

In October 1562, Elizabeth contracted SMALLPOX. The doctors told Cecil that the Queen would not survive. Though her face was left permanently scarred, Elizabeth recovered. Had she died, there would have been a serious crisis. There was a three-way split in the Privy Council about what to do in the event of the Queen's death and later, once she had recovered, Parliament urged Elizabeth to marry or nominate an heir. She would do neither, claiming that she would marry only when the time was right and that to nominate a 'second person' would place her in danger.

The problem was not a shortage, but a surplus, of potential heirs. There were two main claims – the Stuart claim and the Suffolk claim. Various pamphlets were written promoting the different possibilities. Henry VIII's will had confused matters. It had stated that should his three children die without heirs, the throne would pass to the descendants of his younger sister, Mary, the Duchess of Suffolk. Her granddaughter, Lady Jane Grey, had already been executed for attempting to seize the throne in 1553, but there were still two younger girls, Lady Catherine and Lady Mary. Both were Protestants and both were seen as potential heirs to Elizabeth.

However, technically, Elizabeth's other cousin, Mary, Queen of Scots, had a stronger claim to the English throne than the Greys, as she was descended from Henry VIII's older sister, who had married into the Scottish Royal Family. However, Mary, Queen of Scots was a controversial claimant, having been brought up in France and being a devout Catholic. At one point, Elizabeth considered having her favourite Dudley marry the Queen of Scots as a way of bringing her under English influence. Mary, however, saw Dudley as socially inferior and the plans came to nothing. Instead, much to the anger of Elizabeth, Mary strengthened her already convincing claim to the English throne by marrying her cousin, Lord Darnley, and uniting two Stuart claims for any children they might have.

Although neither of the Grey sisters were particularly inspiring candidates, in 1561 Elizabeth appeared to be warming to the idea of making Catherine Grey her official heir. When the Queen discovered that Catherine had secretly married the Earl of Hertford without her permission and fallen pregnant, she was furious. Elizabeth had her cousin imprisoned in the Tower of London for the rest of her life and Catherine possibly starved herself to death in despair. Catherine and Hertford had two sons, both born in prison, but they were declared illegitimate and barred from the succession. Catherine's younger sister, Mary, also married without Elizabeth's permission and she too was placed under house arrest, dying childless a little over a decade later.

## SOURCE 10

Bishop Jewel reflecting on the worries about the succession in 1562.

*Oh, how wretched are we, who cannot tell under what sovereign we are to live.*

## THINK

6   Why was there so much concern about the succession in the 1560s?

7   Study Figure 11 and the text. Who had the best claim to be Elizabeth's heir?

## FIGURE 11

Simplified family tree showing Elizabeth's possible successors.

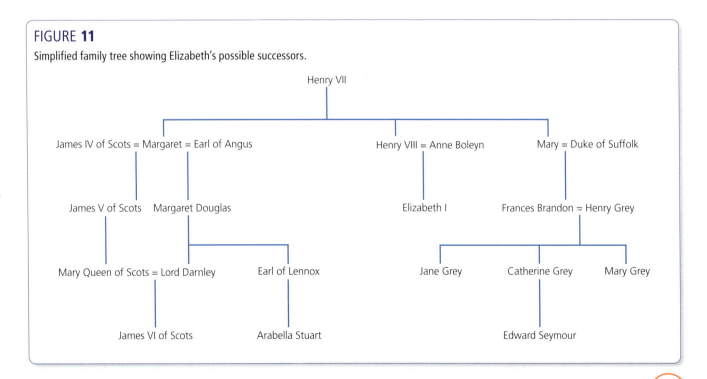

## SOURCE 12

From *The Virgin Queen* by Christopher Hibbert (1990).

*The Councillors gathered round her bed to ask if she agreed that her cousin, James VI of Scotland, Mary's son, should succeed her. Cecil and the Council had already made all the necessary arrangements; but the Queen, allowing the negotiations to go ahead while pretending not to know of them, had refused to commit herself till now. She found difficulty talking, and asked for something to rinse her throat. But the Councillors said she had no need to speak: she had merely to indicate with her hand if she accepted him. The question was asked and she gave what was taken to be a sign of consent.*

## THINK

8  Read Source 12. Did Elizabeth choose her successor?

## PRACTICE QUESTIONS

### INTERPRETATION A

'Marriage and motherhood would deprive her temporarily – perhaps permanently – of the authority and power to rule. To share power she would hate. To renounce it she would find intolerable.'

J. Hurstfield, *Elizabeth and the Unity of England*, 1960

1  How convincing is Interpretation A about Elizabeth's reasons not to marry?
2  Write an account of Elizabeth's handling of the 'marriage question'.

## TIP

Make sure you can identify several people whom Elizabeth could have married and explain why she chose to remain single.

## KEYWORDS

Make sure you know what these words mean and are able to use them confidently in your own writing. See the glossary on page 94 for definitions.
- Cult
- Queen Regnant
- Regent
- Suitor

# Resolution

By the end of Elizabeth's reign, the succession crisis had resolved itself, almost by accident, as most of the eligible contenders had died. The obvious heir was the Scottish King, James VI, the only child of Mary, Queen of Scots. James had a doubly strong claim, as both his mother and his father were grandchildren of Elizabeth's aunt, Margaret Tudor. Although some suggested James' cousin, Arabella Stuart, as an alternative, by the 1590s James' superior claim was recognised by the Cecils and it was accepted that James would succeed. Although Elizabeth refused to officially name James as her heir, even she sent teasing letters hinting that he might succeed her. Crucially, as the end of Elizabeth's life drew near, Robert Cecil began a secret correspondence with James from May 1601 onwards to prepare for life after Elizabeth. The issue of the succession had dominated her whole reign and caused considerable worry, but when Elizabeth died in March 1603, Cecil had arranged for an easy transition. A messenger left London, reaching Edinburgh three days later, to tell the King of Scots that he was now also the King of England. The Tudor dynasty gave way to the Stuarts smoothly and calmly, with the whole of the island of Great Britain, for the very first time in history, sharing a single monarch.

## FOCUS TASK B

### Explaining Elizabeth's decisions

You have been making notes about the succession crisis.

1  Use your notes to answer one of these questions:
   - Why do you think Elizabeth decided not to marry?
   - Why do you think Elizabeth refused to name her successor?
   Make sure you can support your opinion with evidence from the table you created.
2  Imagine you are Elizabeth and the year is 1602. You are aware that your life is coming to an end. Write a letter to a friend, in the strictest confidence, looking back on the succession crisis that you have faced during your reign.
   - Explain the succession crisis from your point of view.
   - Include your judgement on whether you made the right decision not to marry and have children.
   - Explain why others might disagree with you.

## TOPIC SUMMARY

### The succession crisis
- In the sixteenth century there was prejudice against female monarchs, who were thought incapable of ruling effectively.
- Elizabeth almost died of smallpox early in her reign without an obvious heir.
- Elizabeth was put under constant pressure to marry by Parliament and the Privy Council.
- Elizabeth had many potential suitors, both at home and abroad.
- Elizabeth decided not to marry, keeping her independence.
- The fact that the Queen was unmarried led to a succession crisis, as she had no children.
- Elizabeth refused to choose a successor from her numerous relatives.
- When Elizabeth died, the Tudor dynasty came to an end.
- Elizabeth's Council planned for the succession of her Scottish cousin, beginning the rule of the Stuarts in England.

# REVIEW of Chapter 1

## Elizabeth and her Government

In your exam you will be set FOUR questions on the British depth study.

**Question 1** will be on interpretations. You need to use your knowledge to explain how convincing an interpretation is. The interpretation could be a picture or a written source. For example:

> ### INTERPRETATION A
> From Elizabeth I by W. MacCaffrey (1993)
>
> *Elizabeth's experience was very limited. Her life had been led almost exclusively in the seclusion of country houses, with only an occasional short visit to the Court.*

> 1. How convincing is Interpretation A about Elizabeth's early life?
>
> Explain your answer using Interpretation A and your contextual knowledge. (8 marks)

For this question, you need to describe what the source tells you and then use your own detailed knowledge to support and contradict what the source suggests about Elizabeth's early life.

**Question 2** will ask you to explain the significance or importance of something. It is testing your knowledge and understanding. You are not writing everything you know about a topic but selecting what is relevant and organising it to answer the question. For example:

> 2. Explain what was important about the succession issue in Elizabethan England. (8 marks)

To answer this question there are many things you could cover but you need to focus on the ones that show the importance of the issue not on incidental details.

**Question 3** asks you to write an account. It is still not 'everything you know'. You are selecting from your knowledge those things that are most relevant to answer the question. For example:

> 3. Write an account of the ways in which the Earl of Essex affected Elizabethan England. (8 marks)

For this question you need to cover a range of events with enough detail to show you understand the different effects the Earl of Essex had at different times. You need to write your answer in the form of a coherent narrative.

**Question 4** is on the historic environment – an actual place. You will have studied, in depth, a site chosen by the exam board. You have to use your knowledge of the site, and your wider knowledge of Elizabethan England to write an essay that evaluates a statement.

Because you have studied in depth there will be so much you could say about the site that you have to be selective. This is why the statement in the question is so helpful. It provides focus. Make sure you use the statement to develop a clear, coherent and relevant argument from the start, and carry it through the whole essay supporting your argument.

---

Consider how what you read in the source is convincing in the view it gives of Elizabeth's early life. Think about:

- How were Elizabeth's experiences limited before she was Queen?
- Where did Elizabeth live before she became Queen?
- Why did Elizabeth spend very little time at Court?

Then, consider how the source is not convincing. Does it exaggerate how limited Elizabeth's experiences really were? Think about:

- What education had Elizabeth received?
- How was Elizabeth influenced by her relatives?
- What did Elizabeth learn from her imprisonment during Mary's reign?

Look back at topic 1.1 in order to see how you could expand on these points.

---

Which of the following do you think you should spend most time on?

- What succession means and why knowing who Elizabeth's heir was felt so important at the time
- Attitudes towards female rulers and how this had affected Elizabeth's attitude to marriage
- Elizabeth's various suitors
- Elizabeth's potential heirs
- The attitude of the Privy Council and Parliament
- Elizabeth's death and how an heir was chosen.

Look back at topic 1.3 in order to see how you could expand on your chosen points.

---

You could include:

- Essex's personality
- Essex's relationship with Elizabeth and his rivalry with Cecil
- Essex's role in Ireland
- Essex's rebellion in 1601

Look back at topic 1.2 in order to see if you can write a paragraph on one or more of these points.

Read the information below, and use topic 1.2 to map out the key points of your possible answer under five headings:

- How it was impressive
- Why it was so important for Elizabeth to impress her subjects
- How Elizabeth changed/developed Hampton Court Palace
- What else happened at Hampton Court
- Other ways that Elizabeth tried to impress her subjects

Then if you are really brave have a go at writing a full essay.

This is a harder question to practise because we don't know what site you will have studied. The nominated site changes every year. However, you can practise with any site. So below you will find a Factfile of information about a very important Tudor building, Hampton Court Palace, and a statement-based question to get you thinking about the site and how it connects to the themes you have studied in Chapter 1.

The key thing to remember about question 4 is that it is inviting you to reach a judgement – agreeing or disagreeing with the statement and using the site to support your answer. For more advice on how to answer question 4, see Assessment Focus, page 92.

4. 'The main change that Elizabethan royal residences demonstrated was the Queen's efforts to impress her subjects and maintain her power.' How far does a study of Hampton Court Palace support this statement? (16 marks)

## FACTFILE

### Hampton Court Palace

- Located in Surrey, it is about 15 miles south of London. It is located by the River Thames, which provided the quickest means of travelling to and from the Palace in Tudor times.
- It was built in Henry VIII's reign and became his favourite palace. Henry VIII lavished money on the buildings, making many additions, including the Great Hall: see photo (B).
- Hampton Court was one of many royal residences. It provided monarchs with a country retreat away from the city. Elizabeth I was a regular visitor throughout her reign. She enjoyed hunting in the extensive grounds. She nearly died of smallpox at the Palace in 1562.
- Elizabeth made very few additions or alterations to the Palace as she was so short of money. Only one bay window dating from 1568 and one of the kitchens, date from her time. It was therefore a slightly old-fashioned building by the end of Elizabeth's reign compared with the grand houses being built by her subjects.

- The Court moved around with the Queen. The Palace contained countless rooms so that hundreds of courtiers could lodge at the Palace. The huge kitchens provided members of the Court with meals and the Great Hall provided a massive space that hosted two sittings twice a day.
- Elizabeth's power was partly based on her ability to impress others with her magnificence. The Great Hall was a grand public space that hosted court festivals such as masques and plays. The Great Hall is hung with priceless tapestries from Henry VIII's time.
- The Palace served as a diplomatic centre. Foreign delegations were frequently received and entertained at the Palace. The Duke of Württemberg, who visited the Palace in 1592, called it 'the most splendid and most magnificent royal edifice to be found in England, or for that matter in other countries'.
- Patronage was important and factions competed for power at Court. Getting close to the Queen was crucial to having any political power. The Queen's Privy Chamber was staffed by women, changing the political role of the Court. The private apartments of the monarch which lay beyond the Great Hall no longer exist.

(A) the main gatehouse of Hampton Court Palace, (B) the interior of the Great Hall.

# Life in Elizabethan times

**2**

This house was built by Elizabeth, the Countess of Shrewsbury, more commonly known as Bess of Hardwick. After the Queen, Bess was the wealthiest woman in England. The palatial house is one of many prodigy houses built during Elizabeth's reign that were designed to make a real statement. Many still stand today and give a stunning impression of style and wealth in Elizabeth's time. It was a time when English literature also flourished, as did bold overseas exploration. However, you won't be surprised to know that for lots of people in Elizabeth's England, life was not so good. This chapter investigates how the lives and experiences of the Elizabethan people were actually very varied, depending on whether they were rich or poor, and on whether they lived in town or country.

# 2.1 Elizabethan culture: A Golden Age?

## FOCUS

During Elizabeth I's reign, England experienced a blossoming of culture – theatre, art, architecture, literature and music – that has been referred to as a 'Golden Age'. How far Elizabeth was personally responsible for this is debatable. In addition, the idea of a 'Golden Age' might be more myth than reality, created by the government in an effort to strengthen a weak regime. In topic 2.1 you will:

- investigate the cultural achievements experienced in Elizabeth's reign
- understand what caused the flourishing of the arts in this period
- judge how far there really was a 'Golden Age' under Elizabeth.

## THINK

1 Look at Source 1. Why do you think an entertainment district might have been established in London at this particular time?

## SOURCE 1

A view of the Bankside area of Elizabethan London, drawn by Wenceslaus Hollar, showing the Globe Theatre and bear-baiting pit. This was the entertainment district of the capital city and had a notorious reputation. Note that the Globe Theatre and the 'beere bayting' pit have been wrongly labelled. They should be the other way round.

## FOCUS TASK A

### Elizabethan culture

Complete a table like this using the information on pages 34–44.

| Aspect | Summary of developments | Key people (and details) | Key places (and details) | What this aspect says about Elizabethan England |
|---|---|---|---|---|
| Architecture | | | | |
| Fashion | | | | |
| Theatre | | | | |
| Books | | | | |
| Art | | | | |
| Music | | | | |

# An English Renaissance

The Elizabethan era saw an explosion of cultural achievement, influenced by HUMANISM in Europe. The Queen and Court set fashions which were then copied by others. London's population grew and at the same time the GENTRY became more important. They had disposable income and wanted to spend conspicuously in order to impress others and earn promotion. This meant that artists, builders, musicians and writers did well, as their work was much in demand. The invention of the PRINTING PRESS in the fifteenth century meant that new ideas could now spread at greater speed. As new grammar schools and university colleges were set up the curriculum broadened and the English became better educated.

English literature flourished, through poetry, prose and drama. Affordable stories called 'chap books' were sold by street pedlars. New architectural styles came into fashion. Musicians such as Orlando Gibbons, Thomas Tallis and William Byrd met with great success. Nicholas Hilliard was a highly successful artist, painting famous miniature portraits of leading personalities including Queen Elizabeth. The mathematician and astrologer John Dee was an influential figure and John Napier discovered logarithms. Historians such as William Camden and Richard Hakluyt started to base their writings about the past on sources, as modern historians do. Science also started to develop, with an interest in the planets and the workings of the human body. Francis Bacon argued that experiments were needed to test scientific theories and the Elizabethan William Harvey later made the discovery that blood circulated around the body. The Queen's doctor, William Gilbert, experimented with electricity.

# The rise of the gentry

Although the gentry did not work with their hands for a living, they did not belong to the titled nobility. Their status and power was purely based on their wealth. The gentry class grew massively in Elizabeth's reign. There were a number of reasons:

- **The Tudors' suspicion of the 'old' nobility:** the Tudors had deliberately marginalised the nobles, who they saw as a threat, by granting very few new titles and excluding them from government. This left a vacuum which the gentry filled and they became very powerful politically. Indeed, many of the key councillors promoted by Elizabeth – including Cecil, Walsingham and Hatton – came from the gentry class. The gentry also dominated the House of Commons, and they gained power locally through their work as Justices of the Peace.
- **The dissolution of the monasteries by Henry VIII:** the monasteries had owned about a quarter of all land in England. Their dissolution had made more land available to buy than ever before.
- **Increasing wealth:** growth in trade and exploration, together with population growth, rising prices and enclosure, all helped many gentry families to make their fortunes. They were therefore able to use their money to establish estates, to build grand houses and to educate themselves.

The gentry's money in turn helped to fuel the cultural achievements of Elizabeth's reign. The gentry were keen to sponsor architectural, artistic, intellectual and literary endeavours, as this helped to affirm their new status in society.

**DEBATE**

- A common perception of Elizabeth's reign is that it marked a 'Golden Age' for England.
- In the past 30 years or so historians have tried hard to challenge this viewpoint as a myth.
- Christopher Haigh's work, published in 1984, led the way in revealing the problems and insecurities that were present throughout Elizabeth's reign.

**THINK!**

2 Why did the Elizabethan period witness a rise of the gentry?
3 How did the gentry help to contribute to a 'golden age' of culture?

**DEBATE**

- Marxist historians believe that capitalism began to emerge in Elizabeth's reign.
- In the 1940s, R.H. Tawney wrote that the reign saw the rise of a powerful and prosperous landowning gentry class.
- The gentry were well educated and used the House of Commons to air their political views. Trade monopolies, the availability of lands that had belonged to the monasteries, the rising population, rising prices and agricultural changes all helped.
- Their rise was mirrored by the decline of the aristocracy over the same period.

# Fashion

The wealth of the gentry also helped drive the development of new clothing fashions. The wealthy used their money to buy expensive clothes in the latest styles (see table below).

**THINK!**

4   Use the table below to identify clothing items worn by the Elizabethan gentleman and gentlewomen in Figure 2.

Then, as now, fashion was an important status symbol. Clothes were considered so important in Elizabeth's reign that some new Sumptuary Laws – called the Statutes of Apparel – were passed in 1574. These laws strictly controlled the clothes people were allowed to wear depending on their social rank.

| Male fashions | Female fashions |
|---|---|
| • Doublet (long-sleeved silk or satin shirt with ruffles at the end) | • Farthingale (a petticoat with wooden hoops sewn into it) |
| • Woollen / silk stockings | • Ruff (a lace collar on a wire frame, worn around the neck) |
| • Trunk-hose (padded out with horse hair to make bulges and cut in strips to give a two-tone effect) | • Undergown (made of silk or satin and heavily patterned and embroidered, with wide sleeves with ruffles at the end) |
| • Jerkin (a colourful velvet jacket decorated with embroidery, fastened up the front with buttons) | • Gown (satin or velvet, sleeveless, and slashed to show the undergown through it) |
| • Ruff (a narrow strip of starched linen ironed into pleats and worn around the neck as a collar) | • An over-gown (a cape with armholes for cold weather or going outside) |
| • Shoes (leather with cork soles) | • Dyed hair with false hair piled on top |
| • Hat | • Heavy white make-up (lead-based and highly poisonous, but made fashionable by the Queen) |
| • Cloak | • Blackened teeth (also made fashionable by Elizabeth, whose teeth were rotten because of sugar consumption) |
| • Sword | • Shoes (embroidered silk or velvet or light Spanish leather) |
| • Beard | • A small hat (designed to show off as much hair as possible) |

## FIGURE 2
Elizabethan fashions

# Architecture

The building boom and development of new ideas in architecture during Elizabeth's reign led to a period known as the 'Great Rebuilding'. Ironically, Elizabeth did not have the money to be a great builder herself, but many of her subjects were. Many new extravagant country houses were built that reflect the wealth and stability of the era. New houses were often built to impress and host Elizabeth while she was on progress. Strong government had an impact on design. Residences no longer had to include defensive features, such as moats and drawbridges, and decorative gardens were planted. The leading architect was Robert Smythson, who was responsible for designing and building some of the most famous Elizabethan houses, such as Longleat House in Wiltshire and Hardwick Hall in Derbyshire (see page 33 and Factfile on page 63). Buildings varied from area to area, depending on the materials that were available locally. Often, these new buildings were either built of stone or brick, and they were designed to amaze all who saw them in terms of their scale and style. Rising food prices had led to increased profits for the landowners and houses that used the latest styles were a status symbol.

Elizabethan houses were very different from previous Gothic styles, with the latest and most fashionable designs being heavily influenced by Italian RENAISSANCE architecture from places such as Florence. Architects focused on symmetry and size. Many houses had intricate chimney stacks and expensive leaded glass in large MULLIONED WINDOWS. However, many manor houses continued to be less classically influenced and built in a more functional style, such as the timber-framed WATTLE-AND-DAUB Speke Hall near Liverpool and Churche's Mansion in Cheshire. Often, houses were built with an 'E' shaped floorplan, perhaps in honour of the Queen.

Internally, the new houses were also quite different from earlier designs. The rooms were now very light, because of the extensive use of glass. Bedrooms were placed upstairs for the first time. The medieval Great Hall was no longer popular. Instead, Elizabethan houses often had a long gallery on an upper floor, which was used for entertainment and to display art collections. Downstairs, although there were still no corridors, the area was divided into separate rooms with their own windows and fireplaces, which gave families more privacy than they had previously had. The houses were far more comfortable than before, with decorative plasterwork ceilings, oak-panelled walls, impressive fireplaces, tapestries and libraries of books.

## SOURCE 3

William Harrison, an Elizabethan, describing the building craze of the period.

*Every man almost is a builder and he hath bought any small parcel of ground, be it never so little, will not be quiet till he have pulled down the old house (if any were there standing) and set up a new after his own devise.*

## SOURCE 4

Little Moreton Hall in Cheshire. Not all Elizabethans built from scratch. Here a long gallery has been added in the 1560s to the top storey of an early Tudor house in an effort to keep up with the latest fashions.

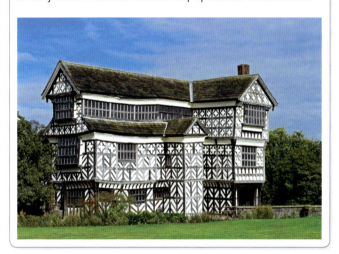

## SOURCE 5

Montacute House in Somerset was built in the 1590s for Edward Phelips, a member of the gentry.

**THINK**

5  Why were so many new houses built in Elizabeth's reign?
6  Add notes to your Focus Task table about fashion and architecture.

## THINK

7  Looking at the text and Source 6, why did the authorities have negative attitudes towards the theatre during the Elizabethan period?

8  Why were so many theatres concentrated on the South Bank?

# The theatre

When Elizabeth became Queen, there were no theatres in the country. So-called mystery and miracle plays, based on Bible stories and the lives of saints, had been popular since the Middle Ages, but they were performed on temporary platforms in open places such as market squares and inn yards, not in permanent theatres. Groups of actors would tour the country to perform, but the government did not like them. Actors were thought to be a threat to law and order, and acting was not considered to be a respectable profession, with actors being thought of as no more than beggars. In 1572, Parliament passed a law that said that actors were to be punished as vagabonds. PURITANS also strongly disapproved of the theatre on religious grounds, associating it with the Ancient Romans and thinking it the work of the Devil. When a great earthquake struck the south east of England in 1580, many considered it a sign of God's anger at the theatre.

A new law in 1572 required all bands of actors to be licensed. The law was brought in because of government suspicion but had an unexpected effect. It encouraged the actor companies to organise themselves and four years later the first purpose-built London theatre opened. Simply named The Theatre, it was a commercial success and this inspired others to copy: The Curtain opened in 1577, The Rose in 1587, The Swan in 1596 and, most famously, The Globe in 1599. By the end of Elizabeth's reign there were seven major theatres in London and 40 companies of actors.

As a result of the authorities' opposition to them, theatres were located outside the city walls. Most were in the Bankside district in Southwark, on the South Bank of the Thames (see Figure 7). The area had a bad reputation, with lots of TAVERNS, bear-baiting rings, pickpockets and brothels. Although crime was common in the area, the performances were exciting, and a visit to the theatre was not just about the play. Theatre-goers could also purchase refreshments, such as meat pies, fruit, nuts, beer and wine, and such visits allowed people to socialise, to show off, to network for business purposes, and to meet prospective husbands and wives.

## FIGURE 7

A map showing London's theatres in 1600.

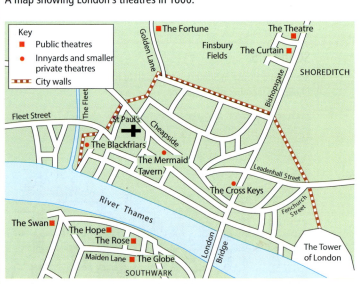

## Design

The design of Elizabethan theatres was influenced by the earlier informal performance of plays in inn yards and marketplaces. The theatres were therefore made up of an uncovered circular pit with surrounding covered galleries. They were also similar in design to bear-baiting pits, as unsuccessful theatres could then easily be converted. As there was no artificial lighting, plays were always staged in the afternoon, with a flag above the theatre signalling a performance that day and a trumpeter signalling the start of the play. A different play would be performed each day. Women were not allowed to perform, so boys played female roles, and the conditions faced by actors were difficult. Behind the stage was a hectic area called the 'tiring house', where the actors would dress in their costumes and collect their props. Some actors, such as Edward Alleyn, Will Kempe, Thomas Pope and Richard Burbage, did well, achieving wealth and fame. Indeed, Burbage eventually formed his own company of actors and became the owner of The Globe.

## FIGURE 8

A drawing of the Globe Theatre based on archaeological evidence.

**THINK**

9    Use the text on pages 38–9 to identify the key design features that are numbered in Figure 8.
(See answers on page 44.)

## Audience

Theatres were enormously popular, with cheap entrance fees making them affordable to everyone. Audiences came from a wide cross-section of society, ranging from poor craftsmen, to merchants, to wealthy nobles. However, the rigid social order was upheld inside the theatre, with the cheapest tickets (costing one penny) being for 'the pit' or 'yard'. Here, the audience – known as 'groundlings' – would stand in noisy and smelly conditions, exposed to the weather. The stage, with its pillars and a balcony, projected halfway into the pit. The groundlings were often badly behaved, throwing food at the unpopular characters during the plays. It was more expensive, at two or three pennies, to watch from the three-tiered galleries, which could seat up to 2000 spectators. The galleries offered the comfort of seating and a thatched roof provided protection from the weather. For an extra penny, a cushion would be provided to sit on. The richest audience members would watch from the 'Lords' rooms' above the stage or even sit on the stage itself.

## Playwrights

Successful playwrights included Ben Jonson, Thomas Kyd, Thomas Dekker and Christopher Marlowe. However, the most famous Elizabethan playwright was William Shakespeare. Tragedies such as *Hamlet*, histories such as *Henry VI*, and comedies such as *Love's Labour's Lost*, were enormously successful. The themes reflected the interests of Elizabethans: violence, romance, magic, the ancient world, exploration and patriotism. There was little in the way of scenery, but each individual play held the attention of the audiences through skilful characterisation, intelligent dialogue, clever dramatic devices, music, varied subplots and even basic special effects. Trapdoors in the stage allowed dramatic entrances and exits. An area of the theatre above the stage called 'the heavens' directed the special effects and 'the hut' provided storage space. Cannonballs were rolled to generate thunder claps, such as in the opening of *Macbeth*. Pigs' bladders filled with blood and hidden beneath clothing were used for dramatic stabbing scenes, such as in *Romeo and Juliet*.

## PROFILE
### William Shakespeare

- Born in 1564, the son of a glover from Stratford-upon-Avon.
- Received a grammar school education, but did not go to university.
- Moved to London to be an actor, joining the Lord Chamberlain's Men.
- Wrote at least 37 plays, mostly during Elizabeth's reign, averaging two plays a year.
- His style and vocabulary has had a lasting impact on the English language.
- Many of his lines have become part of everyday speech, such as 'Mum's the word', 'a heart of gold' and 'a wild goose chase'.
- Became successful and wealthy. The Lord Chamberlain's Men was the only company to perform his plays and became the leading London playing company.
- Regarded as the greatest English writer of all time.
- Part of a partnership who built the Globe Theatre.
- Retired during the reign of James I and died in 1616.

## PROFILE
### Christopher Marlowe

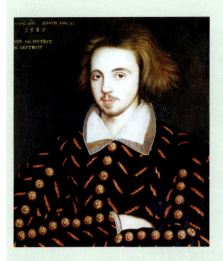

- Born in 1564, the son of a shoemaker in Kent.
- Awarded a degree from Cambridge.
- A poet and playwright, his most successful plays include *Tamburlaine the Great* and *Doctor Faustus*.
- Rumoured to be a government spy.
- Arrested and questioned by the Privy Council in 1593. The reason is not recorded.
- Died in mysterious circumstances in 1593. He was stabbed to death, allegedly in a drunken brawl.
- A major influence on Shakespeare, who became better known after Marlowe's death.

### SOURCE 9

From *The English Gentleman* by Richard Braithwaite (1641).

*Our late Queen Elizabeth of blessed memory, how well she approved of plays, calling them 'harmless splendours of time'. She gave countenance to their endeavours and encouraged them…*

## Patronage

In the 1550s and 1560s actors had been treated with suspicion by the authorities. They were considered to live immoral lives and the plays themselves were believed to be a cause for concern. Performances attracted large crowds, which worried the government in case such groups of people might become disorderly.

However, the attitudes of Elizabeth and her advisors changed in the 1570s. This helps to explain the growth of the theatre at this time. Instead of seeing the theatre as a threat, the government started to see its potential for PROPAGANDA and also for encouraging social stability.

- By the end of Elizabeth's reign, London was a busy and overcrowded city. Its population had quadrupled to about 200,000 people since the start of the Tudor era. By providing entertainment, the theatre could act as a source of distraction for the poor and discontented lower classes, making a rebellion less likely.
- Even more significantly, if the play content was carefully policed, it could influence the thoughts and feelings of the audiences in favour of the Queen and her government.

Some companies therefore won the funding and protection of the nobility. They invited actors to perform in their country houses. Elizabeth's favourite, Robert Dudley, PATRONISED Leicester's Company and her cousin Lord Hunsdon formed the Lord Chamberlain's Men.

Although Elizabeth never visited a public theatre herself, she enjoyed plays and often invited companies to perform at Court, becoming an important patron. Indeed, she allowed one group of actors to call themselves The Queen's Company.

### THINK

**10** How and why did Elizabeth's government encourage the development of the theatre in this period?

# Themes

Some plays contained subtle political messages that were designed to flatter Elizabeth and support her position. They were also carefully CENSORED so as to not be too controversial or to make any obvious references to politicians of the time.

The Elizabethans believed everyone and everything had its own place in a hierarchy called the GREAT CHAIN OF BEING. There was a strong belief that this rigid ordering of the universe should not be changed as this would cause chaos. Shakespeare's plays often emphasise hierarchy and orderliness, and the triumph of good over evil is a common moral. This suited Elizabeth and her government very well.

Shakespeare's history play *Richard III*, for example, presented the Tudors in a very favourable light. It focused on the later stages of the Wars of the Roses, showing Elizabeth's grandfather, the first Tudor King, Henry VII, to be the saviour of the nation. His enemy, Richard, is shown as a hunchbacked, evil monster who brutally murdered his own nephews and many others. In this way, the Tudors are shown to have courageously fought for the good of England and to have won against all the odds.

## SOURCE 10

Lines from Shakespeare's *Richard III*.

Richard's description of himself in the play: '*Richard loves Richard… Is there a murderer here? … Yes, I am… I am a villain… And if I die no soul will pity me.*'

A description of Henry Tudor in the play: '*Thou offspring of the house of Lancaster, The wronged heirs of York do pray for thee, Good angels guard thy battle! Live, and flourish! … Live, and beget a happy race of kings!*'

## FACTFILE

### The Globe Theatre

- The original Globe Theatre was built in 1599 by the acting company the Lord Chamberlain's Men. Six men had shares in it. Richard Burbage and his brother Cuthbert Burbage owned 25 per cent each. Shakespeare, John Heminges, Augustine Phillips and Thomas Pope all owned 12.5 per cent each.
- As with most Elizabethan theatres, it was located on the south bank of the River Thames in the Bankside area. Its name was inspired by the writing of the Ancient Roman Petronius, who said 'all the world is a playground'.
- The building was a timber structure, built of wood taken from the earlier playhouse, The Theatre, which had been dismantled.
- It was a circular, open-air theatre, three storeys high, with a diameter of about 100 feet. It is estimated that it could hold 3000 spectators.
- The pit, around the stage, was the cheapest area to stand in. The more expensive seats were in covered galleries that surrounded the stage.
- The rectangular stage incorporated a trapdoor for surprise entrances.
- Above the stage was a balcony. Two pillars either side of the stage held up a roof called 'the heavens', in which a trapdoor was also incorporated for dramatic entrances.
- The backstage area, the 'tiring house', was where the actors dressed and awaited their entrances. Rooms above provided space for storage and offices.
- The original theatre was burned down in June 1613, when a fire was started by a cannon during a performance of Shakespeare's play *Henry VIII*.
- Today, a modern reconstruction of the Globe Theatre stands about 750 feet from the original site of the Elizabethan theatre of the same name. It opened in 1997.

## FACTFILE

### Shakespeare's plays

A selection of Shakespeare's plays with estimated dates

- 1592
  - *Henry VI*
  - *Titus Andronicus*
  - *Love's Labour's Lost*
- 1593
  - *Richard III*
  - *The Comedy of Errors*
- 1594
  - *King John*
  - *The Taming of the Shrew*
  - *Two Gentlemen of Verona*
- 1595
  - *Richard II*
  - *Romeo and Juliet*
  - *The Merchant of Venice*
- 1598
  - *Henry IV*
  - *The Merry Wives of Windsor*
  - *Henry V*
  - *A Midsummer Night's Dream*
  - *Much Ado About Nothing*
  - *As You Like It*
  - *Hamlet*
- 1602
  - *Twelfth Night*
  - *Troilus and Cressida*
  - *All's Well That Ends Well*

## THINK

11 Read Source 10. Why does Shakespeare present the figures of Richard and Henry in the way he does in this play?

12 Add notes to your Focus Task table about Elizabethan theatre.

### THINK

13  Why did Foxe paint such a bleak picture of Mary and her reign (see Sources 11 and 12)?

14  Why do you think Spenser wrote what he did in Source 13?

It was not only plays that strengthened Elizabeth's position. The government was careful to license the printing presses in order to control what was published. The most widely read book in Elizabeth's reign was John Foxe's *Book of Martyrs*, which was first published in 1563. Foxe was a Protestant and the powerful prose and dramatic drawings in his work demonised Elizabeth's predecessor. Mary's reputation as 'Bloody Mary' owes much to Foxe. The saying that 'history is written by its victors' is certainly true in this case. Foxe's work was designed to flatter Elizabeth and to strengthen her position. The book reflected well on the Protestant Elizabeth, whose accession had seemingly rescued England from the horrors of Catholic rule.

### SOURCE 11

From John Foxe's *Book of Martyrs* about Mary I.

*Mary, having succeeded by false promises in obtaining the crown, speedily commenced the execution of her avowed intention of extirpating and burning every Protestant. She was crowned at Westminster in the usual form, and her elevation was the signal for the commencement of the bloody persecution which followed. Having obtained the sword of authority, she was not sparing in its exercise… Five years and four months was the time of persecution allotted to this weak, disgraceful reign.*

### SOURCE 12

An illustration from Foxe's *Book of Martyrs* showing the burning of Latimer and Ridley.

### SOURCE 13

The Dedication of Spenser's *The Faerie Queene* to Elizabeth I.

*To the most high, mighty, and magnificent empress, renowned for piety, virtue, and all gracious government, Elizabeth, by the grace of God Queen of England, France and Ireland, and of Virginia, Defender of the Faith etc. Her most humble servant, Edmund Spenser, doth in all humility dedicate, present, and consecrate these his labours to live with the eternity of her fame.*

## The cult of Elizabeth

Visual and literary propaganda created a CULT of personality around Elizabeth. The poet Edmund Spenser wrote an ALLEGORICAL epic poem dedicated to Elizabeth called *The Faerie Queene* (see Source 13). The central, mysterious figure, Gloriana symbolises power and glory and represents Elizabeth. The flattery worked! The Queen gave Spenser a pension for life of £50 per year.

People were familiar with the Queen's appearance from her coins. However, from the 1570s onwards a carefully manufactured image was promoted. Elizabeth was short of money, so her courtiers ordered pictures of her to be painted as a means to flatter her and advance their own careers.

The portraits made clever use of symbols to create a mystical image of the Queen. She wore expensive clothing and jewels. Later portraits were full of allegorical symbols. Elizabeth's ministers controlled her image, destroying pictures she disliked. She rarely sat for portraits. Instead a standard face pattern was reused for approved images. Prints based on these were widely circulated.

# An Elizabethan Portrait Gallery

Elizabeth's glorious image was not just a matter of personal vanity. It was a sophisticated operation with a political purpose. The cult of 'Gloriana' was developed in order to make Elizabeth an object of worship for her people.

**THINK**

**15** Study the four portraits on this page. Use the text and your own research to identify the meanings of the following symbols: pearls, gauntlet, eyes and ears, rainbow, angel wings, sieve, pelican, phoenix.

The Phoenix Portrait (A) and the Pelican Portrait (B) are named after the jewels Elizabeth wears in the pictures. They were both painted in c.1575. The phoenix is a mythical bird that rises from the ashes, whilst legend says that the mother pelican pecks at her own breast and feeds her young on her own blood so that they might live.

The Sieve Portrait (C) by Metsys, was painted in 1583 when Elizabeth was 50 years old. In Ancient Roman times, Tuccia, a VESTAL VIRGIN was accused of impurity and proved her innocence by carrying water to a temple in a sieve without spilling a drop.

The Rainbow Portrait (D) was produced near the end of Elizabeth's life. She is wearing her famous pearls, she is holding a rainbow in her hand, her cloak is covered with eyes and ears, her dress is covered in flowers, there are angel wings in the background, an iron gauntlet is suspended mid-air, and there is a serpent on her sleeve.

## PRACTICE QUESTIONS

1  How convincing is Figure 8 (page 39) about Elizabethan theatre?
2  Explain what was important about new ideas and fashions in Elizabethan England.
3  Explain what was important about the gentry in Elizabethan times.
4  Write an account of the ways in which Elizabeth used propaganda to strengthen her rule.

## FOCUS TASK B

### The 'Golden Age'

You have been compiling a table about culture in Elizabethan England.

1  Which aspect of culture do you think saw the most significant developments? Explain your choice.
2  'The Elizabethan Age was a cultural 'Golden Age'. How far do you agree with this statement? Write a balanced answer using evidence from your table.
3  Use your table to write a travel guide for travellers visiting Elizabethan England.
   • Point out the must-see cultural highlights. Give background information and practical advice about how best to enjoy the sights and sounds of the Elizabethan world.
   • There might also be certain dangers to warn the tourists of in order to keep them as safe as possible.
   • Pictures, maps and diagrams would be useful.

## TOPIC SUMMARY

### Elizabethan culture: A Golden Age?
- Elizabethan culture was influenced by the Italian Renaissance.
- Political stability, the rise of the gentry and competition among the nobility all helped to develop a cultural 'Golden Age'.
- New styles of architecture appeared, particularly in house-building.
- Elizabeth and her ministers encouraged the development of the theatre and Shakespeare became the most successful and enduring playwright.
- Government CENSORSHIP meant that cultural output was very closely controlled.
- Government propaganda, particularly portraits, created a cult of personality around Elizabeth as 'Gloriana' and the 'Virgin Queen'.

## TIP

Make sure you can describe the contribution made by three individuals to the 'Golden Age' of Elizabethan culture.

## KEYWORDS

Make sure you know what these words mean and are able to use them confidently in your own writing. See the glossary on page 94 for definitions.
- Allegory
- Censorship
- Cult
- Gentry
- Great Chain of Being
- Humanism
- Patronage
- Printing press
- Propaganda
- Puritan
- Renaissance
- Tavern

Answer to Think question 8, page 39.

1 galleries, 2 flag, 3 tiring house, 4 the pit/yard, 5 stage, 6 balcony, 7 the heavens and the hut, 8 trap door

# 2.2 The poor

## FOCUS

'It was the best of times, it was the worst of times'. Charles Dickens' words in the opening line of his novel *A Tale of Two Cities* perfectly sum up the extremes of wealth and poverty experienced during Elizabethan times. During Elizabeth's reign the poverty problem seemed to reach crisis point. The government's approach focused as much on punishing the poor as on helping them. In topic 2.2 you will:

● investigate why poverty was such a big problem during Elizabeth's reign
● understand what policies were put in place locally and nationally to deal with the poor
● judge how successful the government's measures against poverty were.

## FOCUS TASK A

### Poverty in Elizabethan England

As you study pages 45–52 make a simple spider diagram to record the key information. Include branches for:

● The **causes** of poverty. (Include long-term and short-term causes.)
● The **scale** of the problem and whether it was getting better or worse
● **Attitudes:** how and why people perceived the poor as a danger to Elizabethan society
● What **solutions** were considered to the problem.

## THINK

1 Study Source 1. Why do you think the government punished people for begging?
2 Compare Source 2 with the photos on page 37. How different were the homes of the poor from the homes of the rich at this time?

## SOURCE 1

Beggars being punished in the streets in the sixteenth century. The beggars are being publicly whipped and a hanging is taking place in the background.

## SOURCE 2

From *The Age of Elizabeth* by D.M. Palliser (1983).

*The very poor… in the countryside built themselves one roomed hovels… mean beyond imagination, without windows, only one storey.*

## SOURCE 3

Philip Stubbs, a Puritan, writing about beggars in 1583.

*They lie in the streets in dirt and are permitted to die like dogs or beasts without any mercy or compassion.*

## SOURCE 4

From *The Description of England* by William Harrison (1577).

*It is not yet threescore years since the trade of begging began. But how it has increased since then. They are now supposed, of one sex and another, to number 10,000 people as I have heard reported.*

# The poverty crisis

The Elizabethans thought of society in four social classes. The 'fourth sort', or labouring poor, made up about half of all families in Tudor England. They were illiterate, did not own their own land and spent about 80 per cent of their income on food and drink. Although there were regional variations – the north west of England was the poorest part of the country – there was a growing awareness that there was a national poverty crisis.

# The causes of poverty

The size of England's population had remained fairly stable for the two centuries since the Black Death, but there was dramatic population growth during Elizabeth's reign. The population rose by about 43 per cent between 1550 and 1600. This placed huge pressure on resources, particularly food, and jobs could be hard to come by. With lots of workers available, wages stayed the same, but as demand for food rose, so did prices. INFLATION was a huge problem throughout Europe at this time, not just in England.

Rising prices were not only caused by the growing population. Spanish exploration of the 'New World' in Central and South America had meant that there was more silver in circulation throughout Europe, which reduced the value of all the currencies and pushed prices up. On top of this, Henry VIII had made the problem of inflation in England worse by significantly reducing the value of the coinage in the 1540s in order to pay for his wars against France and Scotland. Indeed, wars were another problem. Whenever wars were fought, taxes were increased, again hitting the poor hardest. Once the wars were over, England was left with large numbers of out-of-work soldiers and sailors who needed to find new employment. In addition, wars with foreign countries often had a harmful effect on England's international trade. England's most important trading partner was the city of Antwerp in woollen cloth. The collapse of this market in the 1550s and later official bans on trade with the Spanish-ruled Netherlands in the 1560s, 1570s and 1580s deprived England of much-needed revenue from its usual export markets. At the same time, trade monopolies were encouraged by Elizabeth and her government to make the rich richer by pushing up prices. They of course always made the poor poorer.

Most Elizabethans lived in rural areas. Unfortunately, agricultural crises and innovations put even more pressure on the poor. This period witnessed several disastrous harvests. There were DEARTH conditions in England before Elizabeth became Queen in the 1550s, and again in the 1590s, which coincided with outbreaks of PLAGUE. With food already in short supply because of the pressure of increased numbers of people, the threat of famine pushed prices even higher. In addition, changes in farming also caused problems. Tenants became the victims of greedy landlords through unfair RACK-RENTING which led to spiralling rents and lots of evictions. At the same time, the growth of ENCLOSURE was also bad news for the poor. The traditional open fields were combined and enclosed with hedges to allow former ARABLE LAND to be turned over to more profitable sheep farming. While good for the rich landowners, sheep farming is not labour intensive, which meant that farm labourers lost their jobs. Enclosure also had the devastating effect of removing the common land. For the landless poor, the common was essential in that it provided them with a place for their animals to graze. For the poorest, a vital means of feeding their families had been taken away.

> **THINK**
>
> 3 Record information from these two pages about the causes of poverty and the scale of the problem in your Focus Task diagram.
> 4 Study Figure 5. Why would an increase in the population cause poverty?

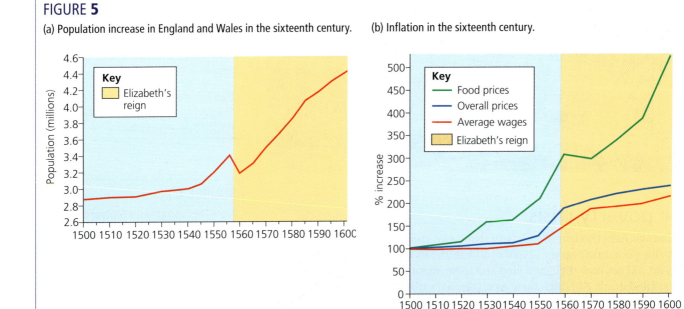

## FIGURE 5

(a) Population increase in England and Wales in the sixteenth century.

(b) Inflation in the sixteenth century.

## FIGURE 6

Harvests, 1500–1600.

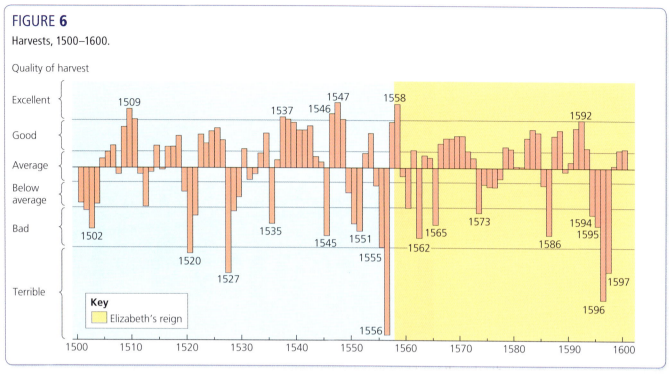

## SOURCE 7

Arable farming before enclosure.

## SOURCE 8

Sheep farming after enclosure.

**THINK**

5   Study Figure 6. Why might bad harvests cause a rise in poverty?
6   Compare Sources 7 and 8. Why might enclosure have caused more poverty?

47

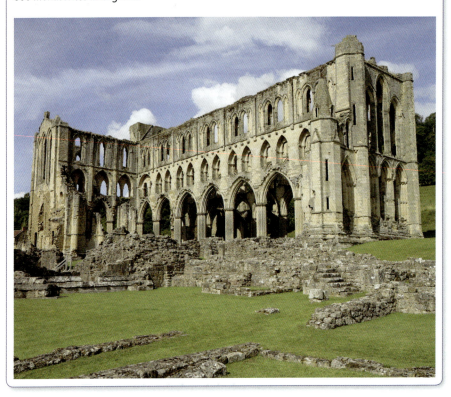

The ruins of Rievaulx Abbey in North Yorkshire. Before the dissolution, there were more than 800 monasteries in England.

7   What is the link between Henry VIII closing the monasteries and the Elizabethan problem of poverty?

In the past, the MONASTERIES had been a key source of charity for the poor. They had provided food, shelter and medical care to the needy. However, Henry VIII had dissolved the monasteries in the 1530s, so removing this traditional source of help. Facing considerable hardship, poor people flocked in ever greater numbers to the towns looking for a better life. Unfortunately, the towns could not cope with such numbers. The migration of so many people brought the issue of poverty to public attention. This forced the authorities to respond and take responsibility for the welfare of the people for the first time.

## Attitudes towards the poor

The Elizabethans believed that the poor could be put into groups, only some of which deserved help. The 'impotent poor' were unable to provide for themselves because they were too young, too old or too ill to do so. They were not to blame for their situation and the government was sympathetic, believing they deserved help. In contrast, the 'idle poor' were seen as a major threat to the social order. There was a belief that there was enough work for everyone. The 'idle poor' were dishonest and VAGABONDS, and often referred to as 'sturdy beggars'. These homeless people were considered to be an immoral and criminal class, perfectly fit but too lazy to find work and happy to live off begging and petty crime.

People were very worried about the 'idle poor'. They seemed to be getting out of hand and townspeople hated the VAGRANTS and beggars. Many were attacked on the streets. Thomas Harman wrote a book in 1567 giving advice to readers about the various tricks played by different types of beggars to cheat people out of money. He also described their use of a coded language called 'canting'. 'Anglers' could be spotted by the long stick they carried, which would be used to steal clothes from people's washing lines at night. A 'ruffler' looked like an army officer, but actually

## SOURCE 11

An Elizabethan beggar appealing to a nobleman.

## SOURCE 10

From *William Lombarde and Local Government* (1594).

*The poor are exceedingly much multiplied because for the most part all the children and brood of the poor be poor also, seeing that they are not taken from their wandering parents and brought up to do honest labour for their living. As they be born and brought up, so do they live and die – most shameless and shameful rogues and beggars.*

## SOURCE 12

Some examples of the 'canting' language used by vagabonds.

*'If you clump a cony you can cloy his peck' means* 'if you hit a victim you can steal his food'.

*'I need a bit for the boozing ken' means* 'I need money for the pub'.

robbed people at sword point. 'Clapperdudgeons' cunningly pretended to be badly wounded by using arsenic to make their skin bleed and wrapping their arms and legs in bloody rags. A 'doxy' could be spotted by always wearing a needle in her hat and by the large pack carried on her back in which she kept all her stolen goods. Many pretended to be ill in an attempt to attract sympathy. Many carried sticks, pretending to be lame. 'Counterfeit cranks' dressed in old, dirty clothes and they pretended to have epileptic fits, using soap to make themselves foam at the mouth, while so-called 'Abraham men' pretended to be mad, walking around half-naked and making strange wailing noises.

Such a lifestyle was seen as sinful, particularly by PURITAN officials who strongly disapproved of such lazy and dishonest ways. What was worse, vagabonds did not tend to travel alone, instead moving around in intimidating groups, robbing and terrorising villages as they went. The government and those in power locally were always wary of a possible breakdown of the existing social hierarchy. The possibility of a rebellion involving the lower classes always concerned them. The amount written by local officials about the 'idle poor' proves how afraid the authorities were.

Disease was also widespread at this time. There were major outbreaks of plague in 1563, 1583 to 1586 and 1590 to 1593, on top of other illnesses such as smallpox and influenza. The wandering poor were seen as a large part of the problem, helping to spread illness around the country. Nevertheless, there was a lot of spreading of alarm, and it has been suggested that many writers of the time, such as William Harrison and Thomas Harman, exaggerated the problem.

## SOURCE 13

From a letter written in September 1596 by Edward Hext, a Somerset JP, to Lord Burghley.

*I do not see how it is possible for the country to bear the burdens of the thievings of the infinite numbers of the wicked, wandering idle people of the land. Though they labour not, they live idly in the alehouses day and night, eating and drinking excessively.*

### THINK

8   In Source 10, what opinion does Lombarde have of the poor?

9   How would townspeople have felt if they overheard beggars talking in code as in Source 12?

10  Why were local officials such as Edward Hext (Source 13) so concerned about the poor?

11  Summarise Elizabethan attitudes towards the poor in your Focus Task diagram.

**SOURCE 14**

An extract from the records of the law courts in Middlesex.

*Thomas Mayard, Oswald Thompson and John Barres, incorrigible vagrants without any lawful means of livelihood, were sentenced to be hung.*

**THINK**

**12** Read Source 14. Why do you think such harsh punishments existed for vagrants?

# Government policies

Elizabeth believed she had more important issues to focus on. She and her government were reluctant to accept that poverty was a national problem and that the government was responsible for dealing with it. The government introduced various measures in an effort to solve the poverty problem indirectly. Early in her reign, Elizabeth carried out a full RECOINAGE, which had been planned by her sister Mary. This helped for a time, slowing down the rate of inflation caused by her father's previous DEBASEMENT of the coinage. A law in 1563 called the Statute of Artificers also placed wage limits on skilled workers, in an effort to slow down the rate of inflation. Her government also tried to slow down the trend for enclosure to protect rural jobs through a law called the Act on Husbandry and Tillage in 1598.

## Local measures

Town councils, such as that in Norwich, England's second-largest city, introduced experimental measures locally to try to deal with poverty. ALMS were collected for the poor, CENSUSES were carried out to make registers of the poor, work was provided for the unemployed in a WORKHOUSE, and efforts were made to control begging by making rules. Hospitals were also set up. In London, for example, several hospitals were established: St Bartholomew's for the sick, St Thomas' for the elderly, Christ's Hospital for orphans and Bethlehem Hospital ('Bedlam') for the insane.

## The Elizabethan Poor Law

The government was impressed by these local measures and gradually realised that a national system was needed to tackle the problem across the country. Until now, government measures had been haphazard and confused. Under Elizabeth, LEGISLATION regarding the poor was passed in 1563, 1572 and 1576. However, by the 1590s, the country's economy was weak and poverty was still a problem. Years of war with Spain had been expensive and the harvest had failed repeatedly. As a result, food prices were at an all-time high and people were starving to death. England seemed at risk of rebellion, so Elizabeth, her advisors and Parliament decided to act. They drew together previous legislation into one clear, nationwide, compulsory system. A Poor Law was passed in 1597, which was later amended in 1601 in what was known in full as the Act for the Relief of the Poor.

Although charitable giving was still encouraged, the new Poor Law stated that everyone had to pay towards a local POOR RATE. People who refused to pay the tax could be fined or imprisoned. This local tax would pay towards parish officials, the setting up of workhouses and the payment of relief to the 'deserving poor'. The Poor Law compelled each parish to appoint four 'Overseers of the Poor'. The Overseers would have a range of responsibilities in bringing in the new legislation. They were to ensure that orphans had apprenticeships, paid for by the parish, so they learned a trade. Almshouses were also to be provided for the old and ill to live in and they could receive handouts of money, food and clothing. This was called 'outdoor relief'.

**SOURCE 15**

From the diary of the Duke of Stettin from 1602. He was travelling in England, having come from the Baltic, and discusses his impressions of England in this entry.

*It is a pleasure to go about for one is not molested or accosted by beggars, who are elsewhere so frequently met with in places of this kind. For in all England they do not suffer any beggars… Every parish cares for its poor… their wants being cared for, till at last they reach their home.*

The 1576 law had stated that there was a third class of poor: those who were able bodied and genuinely unable to find work. The 1601 Poor Law continued to recognise this category of people who wanted to work but were unable to find it. Overseers had to provide tools and stocks of raw materials such as HEMP, wool, wood and iron, paid for from the poor rate. These materials could then be used in a 'House of Industry' or workhouse to provide the able-bodied poor with employment, with their wages paid out of the poor rate until they were able to find alternative employment.

However, there was still a strong belief that many of those in poverty were lazy and much of the legislation focused on preventing laziness by punishing those who were able, but unwilling, to work. Begging was strictly forbidden. The laws stated that beggars would be punished through whipping 'til his back be bloody', after which they would be sent home to their place of birth. Alternatively, they could be imprisoned and put to work in a 'House of Correction'. Some were sent away to work on GALLEY warships. Persistent beggars, as had been outlined by earlier legislation, would be hanged.

# Conclusions

The Elizabethan Poor Law was an important milestone. For the very first time in England, the government took direct responsibility for the welfare of the people. This filled the gap that had been left by the monasteries a generation earlier. Many have said that in doing this, England was ahead of its time. Perhaps a sign of its success is that the 1601 Poor Law lasted. Remarkably, it remained in use for over two hundred years, until 1834. However, Elizabeth and her government's motives were complex. Their decision to establish the Poor Law was not selfless, it was a clever move politically. Again, as a mark of its success, no rebellion caused by poverty occurred during Elizabeth's reign. In this sense, the laws achieved their main aim: social order was preserved. Nevertheless, some have argued that the extent of the problem of poverty itself in this period has been wildly exaggerated, so giving the Elizabeth Poor Law more credit than it really deserves. On the other hand, some argue that the Poor Law did not go far enough. Poverty continued to increase after the Poor Law was introduced and some argue that it was unnecessarily harsh, focusing too much on punishment rather than supporting those in need.

## SOURCE 16

From *England and Wales under the Tudors* by Sinclair Atkins (1975).

*[The] Tudor poor law was more impressive on paper than in fact. Careful study of parish accounts for Elizabeth's reign has shown that a poor rate was levied only in times of dire emergency... It was private charity that bore almost the entire burden of poor relief right down to 1660... It has been estimated that down to 1660 only seven per cent of the money devoted to poor relief was raised by taxation.*

**FACTFILE**

**The main provisions of the Elizabethan Poor Law**

- The 'impotent poor' were to be cared for in almshouses or poorhouses.
- The 'able-bodied poor' were to be set to work in a workhouse or 'House of Industry'.
- The 'idle poor' were to be sent to a bridewell or 'House of Correction'.

**THINK**

13 Add these 'solutions' to your Focus Task diagram.
14 How successful was the Elizabethan Poor Law?

## 2.2 The poor

**TIP**

Make sure you can identify:
- several reasons for the growth of poverty in this period
- several ways that Elizabeth's government tackled the problem.

**FOCUS TASK B**

### How successfully did Elizabeth deal with the problem of poverty?

You have been compiling a diagram to summarise the problem of poverty in Elizabethan England.

1 One branch of your diagram deals with causes of poverty. These causes were complex and interconnected. Which do you think were the two most significant causes? Explain your choice.

2 Imagine it is 1603. You have been asked by the Privy Council to write a report on how successful the various solutions have been in dealing with the poverty crisis. You should include two sections:
- Praise: describe the successes and why they succeeded.
- Criticisms: point out any measures that have not succeeded and suggest improvements where you can.

Use your diagram and the sources in this topic to help you.

**KEYWORDS**

Make sure you know what these words mean and are able to use them confidently in your own writing. See the glossary on page 94 for definitions.
- Alms
- Arable land
- Dearth
- Debasement
- Enclosure
- Inflation
- Legislation
- Monasteries
- Monopolies
- Plague
- Poor rate
- Puritan
- Vagabond
- Workhouse

**PRACTICE QUESTIONS**

1 How convincing is Source 16 (page 51) about the success of the Elizabethan Poor Law?

2 Explain what was important about population growth in the Elizabethan period.

3 Write an account of the ways in which poverty affected Elizabethan England.

**TOPIC SUMMARY**

### The poor
- This was a period of massive population growth and high inflation.
- About half of England's population were poor.
- Many people were moving from the countryside to the towns.
- Elizabethans drew a distinction between the 'deserving' and 'undeserving' poor.
- At the time people believed that there was a poverty crisis.
- Poverty was a threat to social order, and many feared a large-scale rebellion.
- Various laws came together in the Elizabethan Poor Law of 1601, which remained in place until the nineteenth century.

# 2.3 Elizabethan exploration

## FOCUS

A number of so-called English 'sea dogs' led voyages of exploration in the Elizabethan period, adding to the idea of a 'Golden Age'. The sixteenth century was a time of great exploration across the globe, when maps were made of newly discovered lands and world trade expanded. This was partly a result of rivalry between the European powers and the competition led to dangerous hostilities. In topic 2.3 you will:

- investigate the reasons for exploration at this time
- discover who the key explorers were and learn about the journeys they undertook
- judge how far England benefited from this exploration.

### THINK

1 Examine Source 1. Why do you think there was so much interest in exploration at this time?

### FOCUS TASK A

#### Elizabethan exploration

As you study pages 53–60, draw a mind map to summarise the key features of Elizabethan exploration. You could start off with these three branches:

- **Causes** – reasons that the Elizabethans became great explorers
- **Achievements** – with specific examples
- **Consequences** – how the explorations affected England's reputation or wealth.

## Trade with the East

At the start of the fifteenth century, much of the world as we know it had yet to be discovered by Europeans. It was believed that the world was flat and that the Mediterranean lay at its centre. However, there were trade links beyond Europe as there was great demand for luxury goods from the East including spices, incense, silks, cottons and perfumes. Such items were highly prized because transporting them took so long and was so expensive. They were brought from the Far East over land on the backs of camels. It could take two or three years for the goods to reach the Italian trading centres of Genoa and Venice.

These difficulties in trading with the East were made worse by Ottoman expansion. The OTTOMAN EMPIRE was Muslim and hostile to Christian Europe. The Ottoman Turks had conquered much of Eastern Europe and now held power in the Mediterranean. The Ottomans placed high taxes on all goods passing through their territory. This annoyed the Europeans, who were also aware that the Turks had the ability to block off trade between Europe and the East altogether. The Europeans therefore wanted to find an alternative route, which would remove the need to pass through Ottoman lands. Ships also had the advantage of being able to carry far more than camels, so it was hoped that new sea routes would mean that more goods from the East could be imported for less money.

### SOURCE 1

The title page of a book about English voyages and discoveries by Richard Hakluyt. It was first published in 1589.

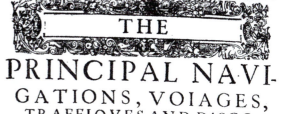

THE

PRINCIPAL NAVI-
GATIONS, VOIAGES,
TRAFFIQVES AND DISCO-
ueries of the English Nation, made by Sea
or ouer-land, to the remote and farthest di-
stant quarters of the Earth, at any time within
the compasse of these 1500. yeeres: Deuided
into three seuerall Volumes, according to the
positions of the Regions, whereunto
they were directed.

This first Volume containing the woorthy Discoueries,
&c. of the English toward the North and Northeast by sea,
as of Lapland, Scrikfinia, Corelia, the Baie of S. Nicolas, the Isles of Col-
goieue, Vaigatz, and Noua Zembla, toward the great riuer Ob,
with the mighty Empire of Russia, the Caspian sea, Geor-
gia, Armenia, Media, Persia, Boghar in Bactria,
and diuers kingdoms of Tartaria:

Together with many notable monuments and testimo-
nies of the ancient forren trades, and of the warrelike and
other shipping of this realme of England in former ages.

VVhereunto is annexed also a briefe Commentarie of the true
state of Island, and of the Northren Seas and
lands situate that way.

And lastly, the memorable defeate of the Spanish huge
Armada, Anno 1588. and the famous victorie
atchieued at the citie of Cadiz, 1596.
are described.

By RICHARD HAKLVYT Master of
Artes, and sometime Student of Christ-
Church in Oxford.

Imprinted at London by GEORGE
BISHOP, RALPH NEWBERIE
and ROBERT BARKER.
1598.

**THINK**

2 How did Spain and Portugal benefit from the agreement outlined in Source 2?

### SOURCE 2

From *The Tudor Century* by Ian Dawson (1993).

*As long ago as 1494 Spain and Portugal had agreed [to dividing] the 'New World' between themselves. Other nations were intruders, to be dealt with as enemies.*

# New ideas and new inventions

Exploration was also spurred on by new ideas. This was the age of the RENAISSANCE, which encouraged learning and also a spirit of adventure. There was a growing belief in intellectual circles that the world was in fact round, not flat. It was therefore suggested that perhaps ships could sail north around Russia, or south around Africa, or west across the Atlantic in order to reach the Far East. New inventions also prompted the growth in exploration. The PRINTING PRESS now meant that maps and other geographical literature were more readily available than before. The ASTROLABE meant that a ship's position could be plotted accurately and the magnetic compass was developed. There had also been developments in ship design. Smaller ships called caravels and carracks were used for exploration and the invention of the rudder gave the crew more control when steering the ship. The triangular lateen sail (copied from Arab ships) meant that ships could now sail whichever way they wished, whatever the wind direction.

# European explorers and the New World

As a result of these demands and developments, various European explorers made discoveries in the late fifteenth and early sixteenth centuries. Many explorers were funded by monarchs who were keen for national glory.

## To the East

In 1487 the Portuguese navigator Bartholomew Diaz sailed around the southern tip of Africa – later called the Cape of Good Hope. Although Diaz's crew forced him to turn around, this journey was crucial in proving that ships could sail around Africa without falling off the end of the world. Eleven years later, fellow Portuguese explorer Vasco da Gama followed Diaz's route but carried on further, eventually reaching India. This opened up a totally new route to India, meaning it was no longer necessary for goods to pass through Ottoman land before reaching Europe.

## To the West

In 1492, Christopher Columbus inadvertently discovered what was called the NEW WORLD. He had sailed westwards across the Atlantic Ocean, sponsored by the Spanish monarchs Ferdinand and Isabella, in search of an alternative route to India. Landing in the Caribbean, he called the islands he discovered the West Indies. Five years after Columbus' voyage, John Cabot also sailed across the Atlantic, funded by England's King Henry VII. He reached what is now Newfoundland in Canada. The following year, Amerigo Vespucci, at the invitation of the King of Portugal, also sailed across the Atlantic and he explored the eastern coast of South America. He decided that this land was in fact a new continent, not the eastern edges of Asia as Columbus had thought. The word 'America' is derived from his forename. The next major achievement was the first CIRCUMNAVIGATION of the globe. This was a Spanish-funded expedition led by the Portuguese sailor Ferdinand Magellan and took place between 1519 and 1522.

## The European Empires

Spain and Portugal clearly dominated the world of exploration at this point, and became enormously rich and powerful as a result. They both began to establish overseas EMPIRES and oversaw the beginnings of the transatlantic slave trade. The Spanish had rapidly defeated local peoples in Central and South America and set up COLONIES there. These areas had large amounts of silver and gold, as well as other resources such as tobacco, potatoes and tomatoes. The Portuguese, meanwhile, colonised coastal areas of West Africa, India and Brazil. In Brazil, they grew sugar and cotton on plantations, using slaves taken from West Africa as their workforce.

# The English join in

Apart from Henry VII's funding of Cabot's voyage, there had been little exploration by English sailors up until Elizabeth's reign. However, England was becoming a significant naval power. Aware of England's vulnerability as an island, Henry VIII had been very interested in building up the navy for military purposes. England had 53 warships by his death. Once Elizabeth was Queen, Catholic Spain was very hostile to English interests. They did not allow other countries to trade with their colonies in the New World without a licence, and such licences were rarely granted to English sailors.

## Privateers

The Spanish monopoly on New World goods angered the English, and led to lots of English pirates robbing Spanish treasure ships and ports. Not all of these acts were actually illegal. So-called 'PRIVATEERS' were licensed by Elizabeth's governments to commit such acts against any ships belonging to England's enemies. The privateers' ships were privately owned, financed by merchants and even the Queen herself. Guns were essential. The privateers' would sail past the enemy and fire BROADSIDE, then do the same on the other side of the GALLEON. English ships were smaller and faster than the huge but slow Spanish galleons, which were unable to change their course in time in order to escape such an attack.

## Trading companies

English explorers did not just seek to damage the interests of the Spanish. They also wanted to promote England. Patriotism and NATIONALISM meant they were jealous of Spanish and Portuguese achievements. England, too, wanted its share of the New World. The English economy depended heavily on trade links with Antwerp, but during Elizabeth's reign there was a crisis in England's traditional markets. England was therefore looking to set up direct links with new trading partners. This was an important reason for the English involving themselves in exploration, as is shown by the various trading companies that were formed because of the connections made by explorers.

- The Muscovy Company had been set up before Elizabeth's accession in 1555, after a voyage led by English sailors Willoughby and Chancellor reached Archangel, in Russia (1553). It traded timbers and furs with Russia.
- The Eastland Company was also established. Formed in 1579, it traded timber, tar, canvas and rope with Scandinavia and the Baltic.
- The Levant Company was formed in 1581, trading goods in the Mediterranean, such as currants and dyes.
- The East India Company, formed in 1600, traded in the Far East in silks, spices, cotton and tea.

---

### SOURCE 6

From *The History of England* by G.M. Trevelyan (1926).

*To the men of London and of Devon the unmapped world beyond the ocean seemed an archipelago of fairy islands, each hiding some strange wonders of its own, each waiting to be discovered by some adventurous knight vowed to leave his bones far away or to come back rich and tell his tale in the tavern.*

---

### THINK

3 Read Sources 3–6. What different motives were there for English exploration?

4 Begin your Focus Task mind map with notes about causes.

---

### SOURCE 3

From *New Worlds Lost Worlds* by Susan Doran (2000).

*The voyages were both a cause and consequence of worsening relations between England and Spain, whose King aspired to write 'Yo el Rey' [I the King]' across a map of the whole western world… [Philip II's] monopolistic and Catholic imperial vision seemed boundless…*

---

### SOURCE 4

From *Tudor England* by John Guy (1988).

*Although eulogised as naval commanders, strategists, and imperial pioneers, the Elizabethan 'sea dogs' were motivated by greed not altruism. If a parallel is sought, they were linked in spirit to the plunderers of religious houses in Henry VIII's reign.*

---

### SOURCE 5

From *England under the Tudors* by G.R. Elton (1955).

*[English exploration] was revived in the middle of the century by the trade slump of the 1550s and the ambitions of energetic and enterprising speculators who had already exhausted the possibilities of a land market.*

## FIGURE 7

Map of routes taken by English explorers.

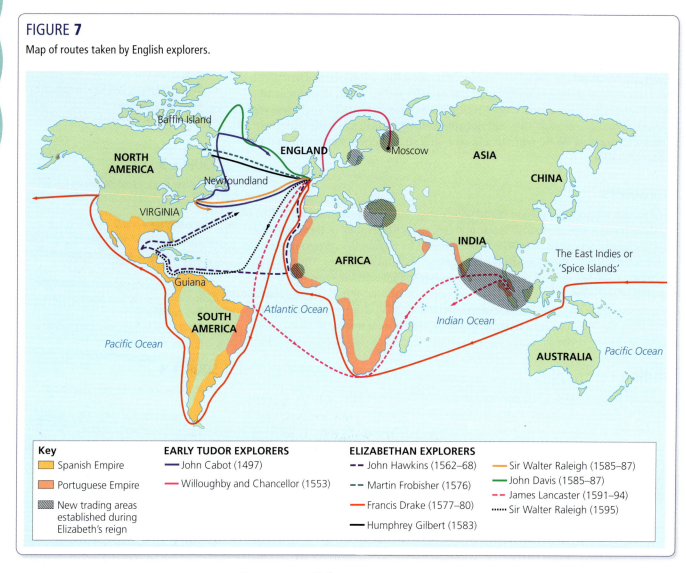

**Key**
- Spanish Empire
- Portuguese Empire
- New trading areas established during Elizabeth's reign

**EARLY TUDOR EXPLORERS**
- John Cabot (1497)
- Willoughby and Chancellor (1553)

**ELIZABETHAN EXPLORERS**
- John Hawkins (1562–68)
- Martin Frobisher (1576)
- Francis Drake (1577–80)
- Humphrey Gilbert (1583)
- Sir Walter Raleigh (1585–87)
- John Davis (1585–87)
- James Lancaster (1591–94)
- Sir Walter Raleigh (1595)

## Route to China

A key English aim, in the interests of trade, was to discover a North West Passage to China. This would involve sailing around the North of Canada. Of course, such schemes were totally impractical, owing to ice in those seas, but the Elizabethans did not realise this. Martin Frobisher attempted this three times, first in 1576, but he failed, as did later expeditions by Humphrey Gilbert and John Davis in the 1580s. James Lancaster met with more luck in reaching the East in the 1590s, taking a route that had been used before. Inspired by the Portuguese explorers of a century earlier, he sailed around the Cape of Good Hope in Africa to reach India and the Spice Islands, after which the highly profitable East India Company was formed.

## Trade with the New World

There was also trade with New World. In the 1560s, John Hawkins made three voyages to the Caribbean, trading slaves he had captured in West Africa with the Spanish colonies. He made a great deal of money, returning to England with gold, silver and animal skins. However, on his last voyage, Hawkins clashed with the Spanish, and lost many men and a number of ships. As a result, he turned to designing new ships for the navy, using his experience of the Spanish attack. On this last voyage, Hawkins was accompanied by his young cousin Francis Drake.

**THINK**

5 Add notes to your Focus Task mind map about achievements and consequences.

# Sir Francis Drake

Drake became by far the most famous English explorer and privateer. He did not just seek personal wealth and glory, but in true patriotic spirit wanted to claim new territory for England. Above all, he hated Spain. As a Puritan, he hated Spanish Catholicism. On a personal level, he wanted to avenge the Spanish attack on his cousin's expedition in 1568. In 1572, Drake captured £40,000 worth of Spanish silver when he attacked Spanish treasure ships travelling from Mexico and Peru as well as capturing the Spanish port of Nombre de Dios in Panama. After this, the Spaniards referred to him as *El Draque*, meaning 'the Dragon'. On his return to England, he was rich and famous, but greater things were still to come. Drake started planning his next voyage. It was financed by a powerful group of people at Court, including Elizabeth I and Cecil. However, they had to tread very carefully, as by supporting Drake's activities, they risked war with Spain.

## Around the world

Drake set sail again in 1577, but it is unclear exactly what he was intending. As it turned out, by the time he returned, nearly three years later, he had circumnavigated the globe. You can see his route in Figure 10. He was the first Englishman ever to do so, and only the second person to do so in the world, after Magellan over 50 years earlier. Drake also returned with an estimated £400,000 worth of treasure captured from the Spanish – amounting to about £200 million in today's money. He himself made about £10,000. The rest was paid to investors, with the Queen receiving a half-share of the money, which was more than her entire income for the whole year. Elizabeth swore Drake and the other sailors to total secrecy about the voyage, on pain of death, as she was afraid of what Spain would do with the information. The delighted Elizabeth rewarded Drake with a jewel bearing her portrait. When the Spanish ambassador demanded Drake's punishment for his actions, Elizabeth responded by knighting him on the deck of his flagship the *Golden Hind*.

## SOURCE 8

An engraving from 1603 of the *Golden Hind* (on the right) attacking the Spanish galleon the *Cacafuego*.

## Sir Francis Drake

- Born in Tavistock, Devon in c.1540, to a YEOMAN farmer.
- A strict Puritan, the family moved to Kent after 1549 rebellions.
- Took part in transatlantic voyages of his cousin Hawkins in 1560s.
- Became famous as a captain and privateer after his successful voyage of 1572 when he returned with considerable stolen goods.
- Circumnavigated globe in the *Golden Hind* between 1577 and 1580.
- Regarded as a hero to the English, he was hated by the Spanish.
- Knighted in 1581, he became an MP in the 1580s.
- Played a crucial role in the defeat of Spanish Armada in 1588.
- His later campaigns were less successful. He died of dysentery in 1596.

## SOURCE 9

A Spanish view of Drake.

*The master thief of the New World.*

## THINK

6   Write an extended caption for Source 8 explaining why English ships were so successful when attacking Spanish treasure ships. You could refer to the text on page 55.

7   Read Source 9. Why did the Spanish have such a low opinion of Drake?

8   According to Figure 10 what was gained from Drake's voyage of 1577 to 1580?

9   How might a study of a replica of the *Golden Hind* help you to understand the work of Francis Drake?

## FIGURE 10

Drake's voyage.

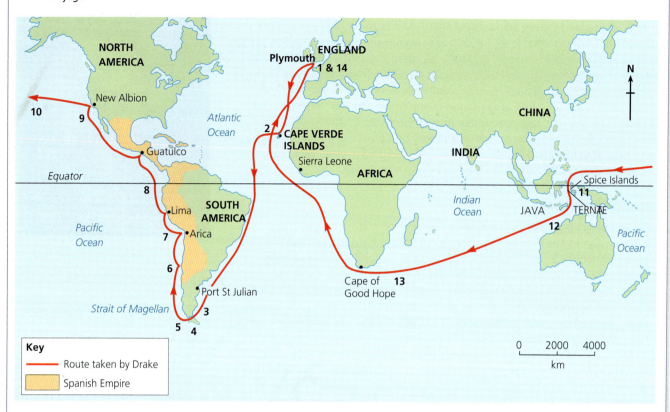

**Key**

— Route taken by Drake

▮ Spanish Empire

1   *November 1577: Left Plymouth with five ships, but returned due to a storm, leaving again in December. The* Pelican *was his flagship.*

2   *December 1577–April 1578: Sailed down the West coast of Africa to Cape Verde Islands, capturing a Portuguese ship.*

3   *April–June 1578: Explored the east coast of South America, but they were attacked by locals when they went ashore at San Julian.*

4   *July 1578: Drake's former friend Thomas Doughty was accused of mutiny and beheaded. Drake put all his men on his three best ships, burning the others. He renamed his flagship the* Golden Hind.

5   *21 August 1578: Entered the Strait of Magellan.*

6   *September 1578–January 1579: the* Marigold *sank and the* Elizabeth *got lost in a storm, returning home. This left Drake and the Golden Hind alone. They landed on the Pacific island of Mocha, where Drake and his crew were attacked.*

7   *February 1579: Continued to sail north, taking Spanish settlements by surprise. Attacked, in turn, Valparaiso, Arica and Callao (the port of Peru's capital, Lima), capturing silver, gold, coins and silk.*

8   *March 1579: Chased the Spanish ship the* Cacafuego, *catching up with it in the vicinity of Esmeraldas, Ecuador. The crew were taken by surprise, capturing its valuable cargo which he offloaded onto the Golden Hind over six days. This was Drake's most famous prize, as it carried 362,000 pesos in silver and gold.*

9   *June 1579: Landed in California, near modern-day San Francisco. Drake claimed the area for Elizabeth, calling it New Albion. Drake was welcomed by the locals as a God.*

10  *July 1579: Sailed across the Pacific.*

11  *November 1579: Landed at Ternate in the East Indies, making a trade treaty with the Spice Islands.*

12  *January 1580: Sailed to Java, picking up supplies.*

13  *January 1580–September 1580: Sailed across the Indian Ocean, around the Cape of Good Hope, up the west coast of Africa. By this point, the ship was running very short of water, which had to be rationed out.*

14  *26 September 1580: Landed in Plymouth.*

## THINK

10  What were the major high and low points of Drake's voyage?

## SOURCE 11

The Drake Jewel, given by Elizabeth to Drake. It contained a portrait of the Queen and the emblem of the phoenix.

# Attempts at colonisation

The courtier Sir Walter Raleigh also led a number of voyages to the Americas. He had received a royal PATENT from Elizabeth to establish a COLONY, just like the Spanish and Portuguese had done so successfully in Central and South America. He named an area of North America 'Virginia' in honour of Elizabeth, the so-called 'Virgin Queen'. It was believed that this area had a huge supply of wine, oil, sugar and FLAX. It was hoped that gaining control of such resources would reduce England's dependence on Europe. Colonisation was also seen as a way of solving the poverty crisis at home, as emigration would ease the problem of over-population in England.

However, both of Raleigh's attempts at colonisation failed: the first settlers faced food shortages and returned home after just a year; the second set of colonists disappeared without trace. A decade after his attempts at empire-building, in 1595, Raleigh set out on another voyage, unsuccessfully looking for the mythical city of gold, El Dorado, in South America. Although Raleigh helped to establish the idea of setting up English colonies in the Americas, it would not be until four years after Queen Elizabeth's death that the first successful English colony was established in Virginia at Jamestown.

## THINK

11 Why was Elizabeth so keen to reward Drake upon his return to England?

12 Use the text to add more bullets to this Profile outlining Raleigh's attempts to establish English colonies in North America.

## PROFILE

### Sir Walter Raleigh

- Born in c.1554 to a Protestant family in Devon.
- A landed gentleman, he was also a poet and a soldier.
- At Court, he rose rapidly to become a favourite of Elizabeth.
- Although probably a myth, he is famously said to gallantly have laid his cloak over a puddle for the Queen to walk over.
- Elizabeth granted him a royal charter to explore new lands. He played a key role in exploring the New World and colonising North America.
- He is reputed to have introduced potatoes and tobacco to England.
- Knighted in 1585 and an MP a number of times – for Devonshire in 1585 and 1586, Dorset in 1597 and Cornwall in 1601.
- Dismissed from Court in 1592 when he secretly married a lady-in-waiting, Elizabeth Throckmorton, without the Queen's permission.
- Temporarily fell from grace but by 1593 he had been released from the Tower of London and was again in Elizabeth's favour.
- Served as the Governor of Jersey from 1600 to 1603.
- Again imprisoned in the Tower of London in James I's reign, but he was released to lead another expedition.
- Eventually executed, under Spanish pressure, in 1618.

## SOURCE 12

From *Drake's Voyages* by K.R. Andrews (1967).

*[Drake] provided in his person a hero-figure upon which public imagination could focus. His remarkable achievement of 1577–80 had little practical effect apart from the immediate gain of treasure, but it did more than any other venture to publicise and stimulate English oceanic endeavour.*

## FOCUS TASK B

### Elizabethan exploration: successes and failures

You have been drawing a mind map about Elizabethan exploration.

1  Do you think that Drake deserves to be seen as an English hero? Explain your answer and explain why others might disagree with you.
2  Imagine you are Sir Walter Raleigh. It is 1598, and you need to make a business pitch to Elizabeth and her advisors to gain funding for a new expedition you are planning to South America. You might mention:
   - reasons for more exploration and what England could gain from the expedition
   - examples of past successes to draw inspiration from
   - examples of past failures to learn lessons from
   - the equipment that will be needed
   - possible routes to be taken.

## TIP

Make sure you can name several Elizabethan explorers and explain three things gained from their expeditions.

## KEYWORDS

Make sure you know what these words mean and are able to use them confidently in your own writing. See the glossary on page 94 for definitions.

- Circumnavigation
- Colony
- Empire
- Galleon
- Nationalism
- New World
- Ottoman Empire
- Printing press
- Privateers
- Renaissance

# Consequences

In the short term, Elizabethan exploration helped to increase the hostility between Spain and England. It made heroes of men such as Drake, and brought great wealth to the merchants and nobles who sponsored the voyages. The glory and riches won for England helped to build Elizabeth's magnificent personal image. In the long term, Elizabethan exploration was the foundation on which Britain's later position as a global superpower was built. Economically, Britain became enormously rich through establishing trading links across the world. Militarily, it led to the development of a powerful navy which dominated the seas until the twentieth century. Politically, it led to the establishment of colonies that later grew into the British Empire, which covered one-quarter of the world's surface at its peak.

## SOURCE 13

Elizabeth I depicted on the title page of a book from 1588. She is shown as the Queen of the Universe. The rings show the qualities attributed to her: majesty, prudence, fortitude (bravery), religiousness, mercy, eloquence.

## TOPIC SUMMARY

### Elizabethan exploration

- Goods from the Far East were in high demand in Europe but difficult to transport.
- New ideas and inventions prompted a wave of European exploration.
- Spain and Portugal dominated, colonising areas of the New World.
- Elizabethan 'sea dogs' were pirates and privateers who stole from Spanish ships and ports.
- Francis Drake was the most famous Elizabethan explorer, circumnavigating the globe.
- The achievements of Elizabethan explorers contributed to the idea of a 'Golden Age'.
- Elizabethan exploration triggered Britain's subsequent rise as a global superpower.

# REVIEW of Chapter 2

## Life in Elizabethan times

Here is another opportunity to review your learning using practice questions. You will be set FOUR questions on the British depth study.

**Question 1** will be on interpretations. You need to use your knowledge to explain how convincing an interpretation is. The interpretation could be a picture or a written source. For example:

### INTERPRETATION B

A drawing of the performance of a play in an Elizabethan theatre.

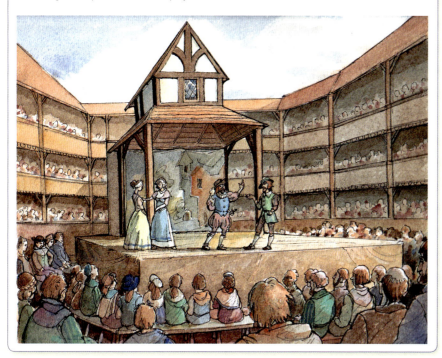

1. How convincing is Interpretation B about the Elizabethan theatre?

Explain your answer using Interpretation B and your contextual knowledge. (8 marks)

For this question, you need to describe what you can see and then use detailed knowledge to support and contradict what the picture suggests about the Elizabethan theatre.

Consider what you can see in the source that is a convincing representation of Elizabethan theatre. Think about:
- What typical theatre design features can you see?
- Why did different members of the audience watch from different areas?
- What sort of atmosphere is conveyed?

Consider how the source is not convincing. Think about:
- Is it convincing that the audience is so calm and orderly? What was it really like to attend an Elizabethan play?
- What were the performances really like – the sights, sounds, special effects, scenery and jokes used to hold the audience's interest?

Look back at topic 2.1 in order to see how you could expand on these points or add your own.

**Question 2** will ask you to explain the significance or importance of something. For example:

> 2. Explain what was important about exploration in the Elizabethan period. (8 marks)

There are many things you could cover but you need to focus on those that show the importance of the issue not on incidental details. Which of the following do you think you should spend most time on?

- The achievements of Spain and Portugal
- English 'sea dogs' and privateering
- Drake's circumnavigation of the globe
- New trading companies
- Raleigh and colonisation

> Look back at topic 2.3 in order to see how you could expand on your chosen points

**Question 3** asks you to write an account. It is still not 'everything you know'. You are selecting from your knowledge those things that are most relevant to answer the question. For example:

> 3. Write an account of the ways in which poverty affected Elizabethan England. (8 marks)

For this question you need to cover a range of events with enough detail to show you understand the different aspects of poverty. You need to write your answer in the form of a coherent narrative. You could include:

- The causes of rising poverty
- The dangers the poor posed
- Government measures to deal with the poor
- How successfully the issue was dealt with

> Look back at topic 2.2 in order to see if you can write a paragraph on one or more of these points.

**Question 4** is on the historic environment – an actual site chosen by the exam board that you will have studied in depth. You use your knowledge of the site, and your wider knowledge of Elizabethan England to write an essay that evaluates a statement.

There will be so much you could say about the site that you have to be selective. The statement in the question provides your focus for you to develop a clear, coherent and relevant argument.

This is a harder question to practise because we don't know what site you will have studied. The nominated site changes every year. However, you can practise with any site. So on the next page you will find a Factfile of information about a very important Tudor building, Hardwick Hall, and some questions to get you thinking about the site and how it connects to the themes you have studied in Chapter 2.

Hardwick Hall is a very good example of the rise of the gentry in the Elizabethan Age. Read the information opposite and use topic 2.1 to plan out an answer to each of these questions.

- Who were the gentry?
- How did they use their wealth?
- Why were they promoted to positions of influence?
- How is their influence represented at Hardwick?
- How representative of the gentry is Bess of Hardwick?
- How representative of the Tudor building craze is Hardwick Hall?

The key thing to remember about question 4 is that it is inviting you to reach a judgement – agreeing or disagreeing with the statement and using the site to support your answer. For more advice on how to answer question 4, see Assessment Focus, page 92.

## FACTFILE

### Hardwick Hall

- Located near Chesterfield in Derbyshire. It is one of many 'prodigy houses' – massive mansions built by wealthy courtiers in Elizabeth's reign. Many were built to host Elizabeth on her progresses, but she never visited Hardwick – it was too far north.

- It was built by Elizabeth, the Countess of Shrewsbury, more commonly known as 'Bess of Hardwick'. After the Queen, Bess was the wealthiest woman in England. The daughter of a gentleman of modest wealth, she became enormously wealthy through her four marriages. When her fourth husband, the Earl of Shrewsbury, died, Bess decided to use some of the money she inherited to build a palatial new house that was designed to make a real statement. It was built on the site of her old family home, where she had been born. The Old Hall was a perfectly serviceable, but old-fashioned building. The ruins of the Old Hall still stand next to the new house: see photo (B).

- Construction started in 1590 and the house took seven years to build. Bess lived there until she died in 1608. Her granddaughter was Arabella Stuart, a potential heir to the throne. She lived at Hardwick too.

- The Hall was designed by the renowned architect Robert Smythson, in the latest Renaissance style. The building has changed very little since Elizabethan times.

- Influenced by Italian architecture, the house is built of stone and its symmetrical main façade is dominated by huge mullioned windows and a ground-floor LOGGIA. A common saying is 'Hardwick Hall, more glass than wall'. See photo (A).

- There are six rooftop banqueting house pavilions with Bess's initials (E.S.) in openwork.

- Proportion was important to the new style of architecture. Each of the main three floors featured a higher ceiling than the floor below, reflecting the importance of the occupants and functions of the rooms. The servants lived and worked on the ground floor. There is a wide, winding stone staircase that leads up to the state rooms on the second floor. There are grand alabaster fireplaces throughout and lots of oak panelling.

- The long gallery, a new architectural feature and the height of fashion, runs the entire length of the second floor. See photo (D). At 50 metres long it is one of the largest examples in England. It was used for indoor exercise, dancing and conversation. There is also a grand room for receiving guests and holding banquets called the High Great Chamber: see photo (C). It features tapestries and a spectacular plaster frieze illustrating hunting scenes. The royal coat of arms also features prominently in this room, to show Bess's loyalty to Queen Elizabeth.

- The building of houses such as Hardwick Hall reflects the increasing prosperity of the nobility, new fashions and the stability of England.

Clockwise from the top: (A) the main façade of Hardwick Hall; (B) the ruins of the Hardwick Old Hall, which the new building replaced; (C) the Hall's principal reception room, the High Great Chamber; (D) the long gallery.

# Trouble at home and abroad

Elizabeth's position was always very vulnerable and her instability was closely tied up with religious disagreements. For some, Elizabeth was an illegitimate HERETIC who had no right to be Queen of England. Elizabeth managed to antagonise both Catholics and Protestants at home. Meanwhile, dangerous plots constantly revolved around her Catholic cousin, Mary, Queen of Scots. Eventually, the momentous decision was taken to have Mary executed. In 1588, in the aftermath of Mary's dramatic death, the Spanish launched their famous Armada, which threatened to destroy Elizabeth and England forever. The portrait here is one of the most famous images of Elizabeth I. This glorious and powerful image of the Queen was painted to celebrate the events of 1588, but in fact masks the truth. This chapter will explore how fragile Elizabeth's position was during her reign.

# 3.1 Religious matters

## FOCUS

Elizabeth's father had broken from Rome, and the English Reformation had created religious confusion and tension. Henry VIII's successor, Edward, had been a fervent Protestant, while his successor, Mary, was a devout Catholic. Trying to avoid these extremes, Elizabeth instead sought to establish a 'Middle Way' in religion. In topic 3.1 you will:

- understand how the Elizabethan settlement tried to reach a compromise in religion
- explore the opposition of both Catholics and Puritans to Elizabeth's policies
- judge how successful Elizabeth was in dealing with religious opponents.

**THINK**

**1** What does Source 1 tell you about Elizabeth's religious settlement?

**2** Elizabeth is reported to have said 'I would not open windows into men's souls.' What do you think she meant by this statement?

### FOCUS TASK A

**Elizabeth and religion**

Draw up a table like the one below to summarise the Elizabethan religious settlement. Fill it out as you study pages 65–71.

| Year | What Elizabeth did | Why she did it | Catholic responses | Protestant responses |
|------|--------------------|----------------|--------------------|----------------------|
| 1559 | | | | |
| 1563 | | | | |
| 1571 | | | | |
| 1572 | | | | |
| 1576 | | | | |
| 1581 | | | | |
| 1585 | | | | |
| 1593 | | | | |

### SOURCE 1

The title page of the *Bishops' Bible*. Elizabeth is depicted in the centre, along with figures representing justice, fortitude, mercy and prudence. At the bottom, a congregation is being preached to and it says 'God Save the Queen'.

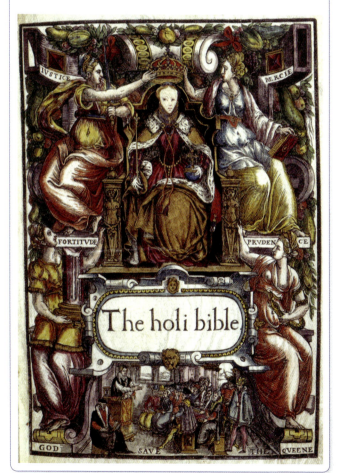

## The Elizabethan religious settlement

Elizabeth was a Protestant. She was Anne Boleyn's daughter, born after the break with Rome. Her education had been influenced by Protestants, such as her step-mother Catherine Parr and her tutor Roger Ascham. When she became Queen, Elizabeth demonstrated her Protestantism by forbidding priests from performing the traditional MASS in royal chapels, so rejecting the old Catholic idea of TRANSUBSTANTIATION. She was also furious when the Dean of St Paul's gave her a copy of the Prayer Book containing pictures of saints, as Protestants like Elizabeth hated the use of superstitious images.

However, Elizabeth was no religious radical. She liked certain elements of Catholicism, particularly church decoration and church music.

### The Archbishops of Canterbury during Elizabeth's reign

- **Matthew Parker** (1559–75). Cambridge-educated, he was chosen by the newly crowned Elizabeth but was very reluctant to take on the role. A moderate Protestant, he had been the favourite CHAPLAIN of Anne Boleyn and had been in hiding during Mary Tudor's reign. He avoided politics and used his influence to try to prevent the rise of Puritanism.
- **Edmund Grindal** (1576–83). Cambridge-educated, he spent Mary Tudor's reign in exile in Europe. Soon after his appointment, he quarrelled with Elizabeth about PROPHESYING. He was suspended and held under house arrest until his death.
- **John Whitgift** (1583–1604). Cambridge-educated, he was passionate about religious UNIFORMITY and oversaw a harsh regime. He hated Puritans and was politically active, sitting on the Privy Council.

### THINK

3   Why was the Elizabethan settlement known as the 'Middle Way'?

### FACTFILE

### The Eucharist

- The main ceremony in Roman Catholic religion is called the Eucharist.
- This is one of the traditional seven SACRAMENTS that give God's blessing to a worshipper.
- It is a re-enactment of the last supper.
- Roman Catholics believe that the bread and the wine used during the Mass turn into the actual body and blood of Christ.
- This miracle is called transubstantiation.
- Protestants do not believe this. In a Protestant communion service, the bread and wine merely represent Christ as a reminder of his sacrifice.

## Aims

Elizabeth's contradictory personal views perhaps help to explain the compromise religion she came up with. Elizabeth's aims were, however, more political than religious. One aim was to heal divisions between Catholics and Protestants before they led to unrest and civil war. This had happened in both Germany and France. The country was very divided. Protestantism was quite strong in the south east of England, but Catholicism was still very strong in the North and the West Country. Another aim was to maximise her personal power and wealth by taking as much control over the Church as she could. Obviously, this did not fit in with remaining loyal to the Pope in Rome.

## Act of Supremacy, 1559

In May 1559, the Act of Supremacy was passed. This dealt with Elizabeth's political aims regarding the Church. It re-established the break from Rome and an independent Church of England. However, as a compromise, Elizabeth chose the less controversial title of Supreme Governor rather than Supreme Head, which had been used by her father and brother. She hoped this would pacify the Catholics who still regarded the Pope as the 'head' of the Church. Elizabeth did, however, require all members of the CLERGY to swear an oath of loyalty to her. The Act also stated that the Church would keep its existing, pre-Reformation EPISCOPAL structure, with two archbishops (at Canterbury and York) and various bishops below them helping Elizabeth to govern the Church. This was a concession to the Catholics, as all the European Protestant churches had got rid of this sort of hierarchy. The Court of High Commission monitored people, and prosecuted those who seemed to be disloyal.

### SOURCE 2

Extracts from the Act of Supremacy, 1559.

*The Queen's Highness is the only Supreme Governor of this realm and no foreign person or state has or ought to have any authority within this realm.*

## A 'Middle Way'

A second law was also passed in May 1559, the Act of Uniformity. This aimed to end quarrels between Catholics and Protestants by making clear what the Anglican Church believed in. It was followed by Royal Injunctions two months later, which outlined 57 rules to be followed, and then the Thirty-Nine Articles in 1563.

The Church created was Protestant. A new Book of Common Prayer was issued, which was moderately worded but contained radical Protestant ideas. Crucially, the traditional Catholic Mass was abandoned. Also, the Bible was written in English, services were held in English and the clergy were allowed to marry. Old Catholic practices such as pilgrimages and saints' images were banned.

However, the law did try to pacify English Catholics. For instance, although the law declared that the altar should be replaced with a communion table, to please the Catholics the law also stated that ornaments such as crosses and candles could be placed on the table. Priests also had to wear traditional Catholic-style VESTMENTS rather than the plain black ones worn by Protestants.

# Catholic opposition and Elizabeth's response

There were still plenty of Catholics in England. William Shakespeare, for example, belonged to a Catholic family. Those Catholics unwilling to accept Elizabeth as the Head of the Church who held public office (as MPs, JPS, judges, etc.) had their positions taken away from them. Attendance at the Anglican Church was made compulsory, but the Pope ordered English Catholics to not attend Anglican services. RECUSANTS who followed the Pope's orders were fined a shilling a week. Attendance at Mass was also punished through fines, and anybody found guilty of performing the ceremony of the Mass itself could face the death penalty.

In 1568, a school for training SEMINARY priests was founded by William Allen in Douai in the Netherlands. The aim was to train English Catholics as missionaries to go back to England and keep Catholicism alive. A year later, some leading Catholic nobles, including the Dukes of Northumberland and Norfolk, led a rebellion in the North, aiming to depose Elizabeth. The following year, Pope Pius V EXCOMMUNICATED Elizabeth (see Source 4). This was very important, as it said that Catholics no longer had to be loyal to the Queen and directly ordered them to disobey her laws or be excommunicated themselves.

## The Treason Act, 1571

As a result, Elizabeth was increasingly threatened by Catholic plots and assassination attempts. In response, a new Treason Act was introduced in 1571. This stated that denying Elizabeth's supremacy and bringing the Pope's BULL of excommunication into England could both be punished by death. Also, anyone who left the country for more than six months had their land confiscated. This was an attempt to prevent English Catholics from going abroad to train as missionaries.

## SOURCE 4

A drawing of the Pope issuing the bull in 1570 that excommunicated Elizabeth.

In nomine Domini incipit omne malum.

The Popes bull against the Queene.

## SOURCE 3

From a report by the French ambassador in 1597.

*As for the manner of their service in church and their prayers, except that they say them in the English tongue, one can still recognise the great part of the Mass, which they have limited only in what concerns individual communion... They sing the psalms in English, and at certain hours of the day they use organs and music. The priests wear the hood and surplice. It seems, apart from the absence of images, that there is little difference between their ceremonies and those of the Church of Rome.*

## SOURCE 5

Extracts from the Papal Bull excommunicating Elizabeth in 1570.

*Elizabeth, the pretended queen of England and the servant of crime has monstrously usurped the place of Supreme Head of the Church in all England, reducing the said kingdom into a miserable and ruinous condition. We declare the aforesaid Elizabeth as being a HERETIC and to have incurred the sentence of excommunication. We do command and charge all people not to obey her.*

## SOURCE 6

From *Elizabeth I* by W. MacCaffrey (1993).

*The Pope had, of course, given [Elizabeth] ammunition by the Bull of 1570, deposing the Queen. It seemed logical to argue that his agents, seeking to secure the allegiance of English subjects to his authority, were thereby conspiring to overthrow Elizabeth and her regime. Hence it was altogether just to execute them as traitors.*

## THINK

4   Why did the Papal Bull (Source 5) make the Catholics a more serious threat to Elizabeth?

5   According to Source 6 how did the Pope's excommunication of Elizabeth place English Catholics in greater danger?

6   Do you think Source 4 was created by a supporter or an enemy of the Queen and why?

7   Add entries to your Focus Task table for: 1559 Act of Supremacy, 1563 The Middle Way (The 39 Articles), 1571 The Treason Act.

## The Jesuits

In 1572, the St Bartholomew's Day Massacre in France occurred. Thousands of French Protestants were killed in mob violence that, it was believed, was brought about by the Catholic government. Bloodshed in France and worsening relations with Spain led to greater hatred and fear of Catholicism in England. From the 1580s, a new Catholic threat emerged that added to these feelings: the JESUITS. This was a religious group dedicated to serving the Pope. Jesuit priests had rigorous training and were sent to England as educators. The idea was to gain influence over rich and powerful families and to turn them against the Queen and the Anglican Church. Once in England, they also helped to smuggle other priests into the country. One of the first and most famous English Jesuit priests was Edmund Campion. He was a brave and charismatic leader. When he arrived in 1580, he first went to Lancashire, where Catholicism was strongest. Later he moved to London, holding church services in the homes of important Catholic families.

All this had to be done secretly, with Campion wearing disguises and using 'safe houses' to avoid arrest. The wealthy Anne Vaux and her sister Eleanor Brooksby were both involved in renting houses across the country for the priests to use. Some houses had so-called priest holes. These were cleverly concealed rooms and spaces where priests could hide and where the illegal Mass could be celebrated. Nicholas Owen, a Catholic carpenter, was particularly important in creating a network of 'safe houses' for priests to use.

### THINK

8  Why do you think Catholics incorporated priest holes (such as Source 7) in their houses?

9  Why was Elizabeth so concerned about Jesuits?

### SOURCE 9

From *Elizabeth I* by Christopher Haigh (1988).

*With the inflow of Catholic seminary priests from 1574, and the arrival of Jesuits in 1580, Catholic resistance was hardening; with a new supply of priests, the old religion was not going to die out – it would have to be murdered.*

### SOURCE 10

A letter written about Jesuits in 1586 by Elizabeth to her cousin, James VI of Scots.

*I thank God that you beware so soon of Jesuits, that have been the source of these treacheries in this realm, and will have spread like an evil weed, if at first they be not weeded out... What religion is this, that they say the way to salvation is to kill the prince...*

### SOURCE 7

A priest hole at Baddesley Clinton, a house in Warwickshire. The house contained three priest holes and was the home of a Jesuit priest, Henry Garnet, for fourteen years. You can just see the priest's bed at the end of the hole. One of the ways holes were reached was by climbing down the hole of a fifteenth-century toilet.

### SOURCE 8

From *Secret Chambers and Hiding Places* by Allan Fea (1908).

*With incomparable skill Owen knew how to conduct priests to a place of safety along subterranean passages, to hide them between walls and bury them in impenetrable recesses, and to entangle them in labyrinths and a thousand windings. But what was much more difficult of accomplishment, he so disguised the entrances to these as to make them most unlike what they really were.*

## Repression of Catholics

Increasingly worried by Catholic activity, the authorities introduced further measures. In 1581 new laws were passed. The fine for recusancy was raised to £20 and any attempt to convert people to the Catholic faith was made a treasonable offence. In 1585 Parliament passed another harsh law called the Act Against Jesuits and Seminary Priests. This made becoming a priest TREASON, and all priests were ordered to leave England within 40 days on pain of death.

The officials who raided the 'safe houses' were called PURSUIVANTS, and their searches could last for up to a week and result in the houses being ripped apart. The Jesuit Edmund Campion was caught within a year of his arrival. He was successfully located by Walsingham's spy network and taken to the Tower of London. Campion was offered his freedom if he converted to Protestantism, but he refused. Even when tortured on the rack, he denied any plotting against Elizabeth, but was still executed for treason in 1581. Some were luckier. The priest-hole builder Nicholas Owen helped to mastermind the escape of a Jesuit, John Gerard, from the Tower of London in 1597.

Further force was used to control the Catholics in the 1590s. Large gatherings of Catholics were made illegal in 1593 and Catholics' freedom of movement was restricted. They were allowed to travel no further than 5 miles from their homes.

## The threat subsides

By 1603, the government campaign against the Catholics had been largely successful at wiping them out as a serious force. It is estimated that perhaps 10 per cent of the population were Catholic sympathisers by the end of Elizabeth's reign, but only 2 per cent were actual recusants.

Not all of the credit for this, though, should be given to Elizabeth and her government. The Pope, himself, was partially to blame for the collapse of English Catholicism. He had forbidden Catholics to attend Church services, but few people were rich enough to become recusants because of the fines imposed by the government. Years later, the Pope annoyed English Catholics by appointing a Jesuit, George Blackwell, as the 'Archpriest' of England, even though he was an unpopular choice. The Pope and Spain had also encouraged plots and rebellions against Elizabeth. Although most English Catholics did not involve themselves in such activities, a few English Catholics did commit treason by plotting with England's enemies. This helped to reinforce the idea that Catholicism was dangerous, unpatriotic and 'foreign'.

# Puritan opposition and Elizabeth's response

It was not only Catholics who were unhappy with Elizabeth's religious settlement. Puritans were also dissatisfied with the compromise. For them, the old Roman Catholic Church was corrupt and too many of its traditions were based on superstition, not the Bible. They found the Catholic parts of Elizabeth's 'Middle Way' offensive. In particular, they were angry about the continued existence of bishops and about the vestments worn by the Anglican clergy.

Like the Catholics, they became a particular problem for Elizabeth from the 1570s onwards. There were many senior people at Court, in the Church and in Parliament who were sympathetic to the Puritans. Even Elizabeth's favourite, Robert Dudley, was a Puritan. Influenced by CALVINIST ideas, which were becoming popular in Scotland, Thomas Cartwright delivered a series of lectures at the University of Cambridge in 1570. He called for the abolition of bishops. He also made no mention of Elizabeth as 'Supreme Governor'. She was horrified at the suggestion that the Church hierarchy should be removed, seeing the idea as being a dangerous and revolutionary threat to her own authority.

**THINK**

10 How did the government persecute Catholics?

11 Why did the government persecute Catholics so brutally?

**SOURCE 12**

The numbers of Catholics executed in Elizabeth's reign.

*1558–76: none*

*1577: 1 priest*

*1578: 1 priest*

*1579–85: 35, including 27 priests*

*1587: 6 priests*

*1588: 31, including 21 priests*

*1590–1603: 88, including 53 priests*

## SOURCE 13

Part of the speech made by Peter Wentworth in the House of Commons in February 1576.

*I have never seen in any Parliament but this last the liberty of free speech in so many ways infringed... The Queen said that we should not deal in any matters of religion... It is a dangerous thing in a [Queen] unkindly to abuse her nobility and people.*

## THINK

12 Why did the Puritans disapprove of the Elizabethan settlement?
13 Why was Elizabeth so worried about Puritans (see Source 15)?
14 Why did Elizabeth quarrel with the Archbishop of Canterbury, Edmund Grindal (Source 14)?

## SOURCE 14

Edmund Grindal, the Archbishop of Canterbury, to Elizabeth in December 1576.

*And although ye are a mighty prince yet remember that He which dwelleth in heaven is mightier.*

## SOURCE 15

A letter written about Puritans in 1590 by Elizabeth to her cousin, James VI of Scots.

*Let me warn you that there is risen... a sect of perilous consequence, such as would have no Kings but a presbytery, and take our place while they enjoy our privilege. I pray you, stop the mouths, or make the shorter the tongues, of such ministers as dare presume to speak out...*

## SOURCE 16

From *The Reign of Elizabeth I* by Christopher Haigh (1984).

*For a decade or more, the Church of England was a Protestant Church with many Catholic churches; for even longer, it was a Protestant Church with many Catholic, or at least conservative, clergy.*

# Elizabeth's quarrels

Puritan printing presses were destroyed in 1572 after two pamphlets criticising the structure and beliefs of the Church were published. Puritan ideas were, however, debated in Parliament at this time. This angered the Queen, who rejected any bills proposed by Puritans. Eventually, in 1576, she stated that MPs were no longer allowed to discuss religious matters without her permission. When the Puritan Peter Wentworth challenged this (see Source 13), he was imprisoned. The Puritan threat also led to a serious disagreement between the Queen and the Archbishop of Canterbury, Edmund Grindal (see Source 14). She was concerned about the practice of prophesying. These were prayer meetings where the Bible was discussed and debated and where sermons were said. Essentially, they were training sessions for the clergy. However, Elizabeth was concerned that such meetings were a dangerous opportunity for spreading Puritan ideas around the country. When Grindal refused to close them down, Elizabeth had him placed under house arrest, where he remained for the next seven years, until his death.

# Whitgift's repression of Puritanism

Grindal's eventual replacement was John Whitgift. He was a strict Anglican who ended prophesying. He also immediately issued the Three Articles, forcing all members of the clergy to swear absolute acceptance of bishops, the Prayer Book and the Thirty-Nine Articles of 1563. The fact that 300 ministers were suspended as a result of this points to the mixture of opinions which existed within the Elizabethan Church. In the same year as Whitgift's appointment, a Puritan called William Stubbs had his hand cut off for writing a pamphlet criticising Elizabeth.

Archbishop Whitgift's harsh approach pushed a few Puritans into breaking away from the Anglicans altogether to become Separatists or Brownists. They were named after Robert Browne, who was imprisoned after setting up a separate congregation at Norwich. Later, scurrilous Puritan pamphlets appeared, published anonymously in 1589. Their coarse language and disrespectful tone shocked many and turned more people against the Puritans. It also gave the government the excuse it needed to attack the Puritans further. In 1593, the government passed the Act Against Seditious Sectaries, which allowed the authorities to execute anybody suspected of being a Separatist. In the same year, Richard Hooker wrote an influential book called *The Laws of Ecclesiastical Polity* that defended the 'Middle Way' and dismissed Puritan criticisms.

# Conclusions

Elizabeth's settlement was very intelligent as it satisfied most people. Her Anglican Church was a Protestant Church that looked Catholic. This cleverly recognised that most English people would be willing to accept some Protestant beliefs if the Church kept its traditional appearance. Elizabeth believed that the 'Middle Way' was the only way of bringing political stability and religious harmony to England. However, not everyone was happy. In spite of efforts by both Catholics and Puritans to overthrow it, the religious settlement of 1559 remained in place.

Elizabeth's claim that she had no desire to 'open windows into men's souls', looking only for her people to seem to have the same beliefs, is questionable. She became increasingly intolerant of religious differences after the 1570s. The government measures applied pressure on those who would not accept the 'Middle Way'. Most Puritans remained Anglicans, and few Catholics were bold enough to be recusants. Extremists were dealt with firmly. Government propaganda was effectively used to destroy the reputations of both groups of opponents, and turn public opinion against them. By 1603, Elizabeth had succeeded in winning over the majority of the population.

## FOCUS TASK B

### Elizabeth's Middle Way

1  Where would you put Elizabeth's religious settlement on a scale of 1 to 5 (1 being strictly Protestant, 5 being strictly Catholic)? Explain your answer.

2  Write a speech.

*The Catholics! Vile wretches, bloody priests and false traitors, here in our bosoms and beyond the seas. We have chopped off some of the enemy's branches but they will grow again.*

This is the opening part of a speech made by Sir Christopher Hatton in 1589 during a debate in Parliament about religious divisions in England. As a member of the Privy Council, he has been asked by Elizabeth to encourage support for the 'Middle Way' by spreading fear and suspicion of religious opponents.

Your task is to finish his speech for him.

Consider including:

● information about the 'Middle Way' and why people should be satisfied with it
● the dangerous activities undertaken by the Catholics at home and abroad
● the dangers posed by Puritans
● what the government's harsh laws against religious opponents were
● why the government's actions were justified.

## PRACTICE QUESTIONS

1  How convincing is Source 8 (page 68) about how English Catholics opposed Elizabeth's religious settlement?

2  Explain what was important about the Papal Bull of 1570.

3  Write an account of the ways in which Puritans posed a challenge to Elizabeth and her régime.

4  Write an account of the ways in which Elizabeth and her government enforced the religious settlement.

## TOPIC SUMMARY

### Religious matters

● Elizabeth's 'Middle Way' brought both Catholic and Protestant elements into the Anglican Church.
● Some Catholics were involved in rebellions and plots against Elizabeth.
● About 300 missionaries and Jesuits tried to revive Catholicism in England.
● Puritans spoke out in Parliament, preached and published pamphlets.
● The government took a harsher line from the 1570s.
● A new Treason Act and various laws were passed by the government to deal with those who disagreed with the 'Middle Way'.
● Nearly 200 Catholics were executed during Elizabeth's reign.
● Religious civil wars did not take place in England as they did in Europe.

## DEBATE

● The English Reformation has traditionally been seen as a political rather than a religious event.
● Historians such as A.F. Pollard (1902) have taken the break with Rome and the establishment of the Anglican Church as a sign of growing English nationalism and xenophobia.
● 'Royal supremacists' argued that England should be an independent 'empire' and that the Pope was merely a foreign ruler who should have no authority over England.
● The Elizabethan settlement ensured that England was completely in charge of its own affairs.

## TIP

Make sure you can explain:
● the roles played by several different people in opposing Elizabeth's religious settlement and
● several ways in which Elizabeth dealt with religious opposition.

## KEYWORDS

Make sure you know what these words mean and are able to use them confidently in your own writing. See the glossary on page 94 for definitions.

● Calvinist
● Clergy
● Episcopal
● Excommunicated
● Jesuit
● Justice of the Peace (JP)
● Mass
● Prophesying
● Pursuivants
● Recusant
● Seminary
● Transubstantiation
● Treason
● Vestments

# 3.2 Mary, Queen of Scots

## SOURCE 1

From Simon Schama's *History of Britain*, BBC TV series.

*Mary had become maximum security threat number one – not just a headache, but a magnet for conspiracy.*

## FOCUS

Although they never met face-to-face, the Queen of Scots was a constant thorn in Elizabeth's side. After fleeing Scotland in disgrace, Mary spent the last nineteen years of her life as a prisoner in England. She was eventually executed in 1587. In topic 3.2 you will:

● understand who Mary, Queen of Scots was and why she was a threat to Elizabeth
● explore the various plots centred around Mary during Elizabeth's reign
● judge whether Elizabeth made the correct decision in having Mary executed.

## FACTFILE

**Mary Tudor**: Daughter of Henry VIII, sister of Elizabeth, Queen of England 1553–58, known as Bloody Mary.

**Mary Stuart**: Daughter of James V, cousin of Elizabeth, Queen of Scotland 1542 –1567, known as Mary, Queen of Scots.

## FOCUS TASK A

### Mary's life

As you study pages 72–78 make notes about Mary, Queen of Scots under the following headings:

● Early life and career
● Treatment by Elizabeth after 1568
● Her role in plots against Elizabeth
● The Babington Plot
● Her execution and responses to it.

## SOURCE 2

The execution of Mary, Queen of Scots. A priest is holding a crucifix so Mary can touch it as she dies. To the left her clothes are burned. She is dressed in red, the colour of Catholic martyrdom.

## THINK

1 What impression does Source 2 give you of Mary's death?
2 Do you think this Source was created by a supporter or an opponent of Mary? Give your reasons.

## Mary's background

Mary was Elizabeth's cousin. She had become the Queen of Scots as a baby, but violence and instability in Scotland meant that she spent her most of her early life in France, cared for by her mother's family. She was brought up as a Catholic and grew into a beautiful and accomplished young woman. After a brief marriage to the French King, the widowed Mary returned to Scotland in 1561 after over a decade abroad. At this time, Scotland was going though its own Protestant Reformation. This was unfortunate, putting the Catholic Mary at odds with her people. Although she was Queen, Mary was very much a foreigner in her own land.

## A rival for the throne?

England had always had a difficult relationship with Scotland, but the situation was further complicated because of Elizabeth's refusal to marry. Elizabeth's childlessness meant that Mary was a potential heir to the English throne (see Figure 11 on page 29 to understand Mary's claim to the throne). Mary was keen to assert her claim and therefore Elizabeth was deeply suspicious of her cousin. Elizabeth had suggested that Mary marry her own favourite, Robert Dudley, as a way of controlling the Scottish Queen. Mary instead took her own cousin Lord Darnley as her second husband. Like Mary and Elizabeth, Darnley was also descended from King Henry VII, and this marriage was designed to strengthen Mary's claims to the English throne. It infuriated Elizabeth.

Mary's marriage to the violent and drunken Darnley was not a success. When he was murdered, after less than two years, there was gossip that Mary had had a hand in the crime. The rumours were strengthened still further when she promptly took a third husband, Earl Bothwell. Bothwell was widely suspected of having arranged Darnley's murder. Civil war broke out in Scotland. Mary was forced to ABDICATE in favour of her infant son.

## Mary comes to England

She quickly escaped captivity at Loch Leven in Scotland and fled to England, arriving, disguised, in a fishing boat at Workington in Cumberland in May 1568. Mary might have been Elizabeth's cousin, but her arrival on English soil was unwelcome news to Elizabeth. Mary was pro-French, a Catholic and a potential heir. Those who questioned Elizabeth's legitimacy even considered Mary to be the rightful Queen of England. Elizabeth certainly did not want such a threat at her Court. She was afraid that Mary could act as a focus for Catholic resistance. She was quickly moved, firstly to Carlisle Castle and then Bolton Castle. Elizabeth chose to keep Mary under HOUSE ARREST far away in the North and the Midlands, in isolated locations far from the coast, and from London and Scotland. In this way she hoped to limit any threat that Mary might pose.

# The Northern Rebellion, 1569

Mary, Queen of Scots' arrival in England triggered a Catholic rebellion. This plot started as a Court CONSPIRACY. The Duke of Norfolk played a central role. He was the most senior English noble, the wealthiest landowner in the country, and a cousin of the Queen. He resented William Cecil's power as Elizabeth's chief minister and was frustrated, feeling that his political talents were under-rated by Elizabeth and her regime. He was also a Catholic sympathiser and disapproved of Cecil's unfriendly policies towards Spain. Norfolk planned to marry Mary and set her up as Elizabeth's heir as a way of gaining greater influence himself and weakening Cecil's position. At this stage, there was no plan to actually remove Elizabeth as Queen. He enlisted the help of a number of courtiers, including two of Elizabeth's councillors. One of these was Sir Nicholas Throckmorton.

### Mary, Queen of Scots

- Mary Stuart was born in December 1542, the daughter of James V of Scots and Marie de Guise.
- Became Queen of Scotland aged six days, but lived in France between 1548 and 1561. Her mother ruled Scotland as regent in her absence.
- Brought up as a Roman Catholic.
- Considered beautiful and intelligent, Mary was musical and an accomplished linguist.
- She married the heir to the French throne and was briefly Queen of France for eighteen months, but her husband, Francis II, died aged only sixteen.
- Mary's second marriage to Henry, Lord Darnley, was brief and unhappy, but produced a son called James.
- Darnley's murder and Mary's third marriage to Earl Bothwell triggered a chain of events that led to Mary's forced abdication in 1567. She was succeeded by her baby son, James VI.
- Mary fled to England and lived in captivity, though in relative luxury, for nineteen years.
- Mary was executed in February 1587 after being implicated in the Babington Plot.

3  Why did Mary's presence in England pose a problem for Elizabeth?

### SOURCE 3

From a report by the Spanish ambassador to Philip II concerning the Northern Rebellion.

*They will, by armed force, release Queen Mary and take possession of all the north country, restoring the Catholic religion.*

### SOURCE 4

Details on the Northern Rebellion from *Holinshed's Chronicles*, a history book published during Elizabeth's reign.

*Upon Monday the thirteenth of November, they went to Durham with their banners displayed. They had a cross with a banner of the five wounds borne before them. As soon as they entered, they went to the Cathedral, where they tore the bible and communion books. They had a Mass, which the earls and the rest heard with such lewd devotion as they had.*

**THINK**

4  What were the motives of those involved in the Northern Rebellion?
5  Why did the Northern Rebellion fail?

Surprisingly, the other was Elizabeth's favourite, the Puritan Robert Dudley (the Earl of Leicester). Dudley was also keen to reduce Cecil's power. However, the guilt-stricken Dudley soon confessed all to the Queen and Cecil. Once Dudley had 'let the cat out of the bag', Norfolk fled Court. When he was captured and imprisoned, Norfolk begged for Elizabeth's forgiveness.

## Rebel success

Although Norfolk had ordered his fellow conspirators not to carry out a rebellion once the plot was uncovered, there were still rumours that an uprising was planned. Elizabeth therefore decided to summon the Earl of Northumberland and the Earl of Westmorland to Court. They were both Catholics and she suspected them of disloyalty. Elizabeth's action was miscalculated, actually pushing the earls into rebellion. On 9 November 1569, the two earls joined forces at Brancepeth Castle and church bells rang out to call people to rebel. The rising involved nearly 5000 rebels who moved through the north of England. They illegally heard Mass in Durham Cathedral on 14 November. They then headed further south, and soon most of the land east of the Pennines was in rebel hands. The Earl of Sussex, the President of the Council of the North, struggled to raise an army on Elizabeth's behalf to deal with the rebellion. By December, the rebels had captured Barnard Castle. They also captured the port of Hartlepool on the east coast, where they were expecting help to arrive from Spain as promised by the Spanish AMBASSADOR, de Spes. The situation seemed very serious indeed.

## The rebellion collapses

However, such international help never appeared. The Spanish were fellow Catholics but were not too keen on the pro-French Mary Stuart. In fact, the whole affair was poorly planned by the earls, who never reached the South. They had not properly mobilised their forces and they had no coherent strategy. The vast majority of English Catholics and most of the nobility remained loyal to Elizabeth. Crucially, the Pope had not yet issued the BULL excommunicating Elizabeth. Had this already happened, English Catholics might have been more willing to get involved in the Rebellion. Key northern towns – Berwick, Pontefract and York – were held by the government. As the royal army moved north, rumours of its strength encouraged the rebels to retreat. After a short battle, the earls crossed the border into Scotland on 19 December.

## Reprisals

After the Rebellion of the Northern Earls, Elizabeth strengthened her control by reorganising the Council of the North and by confiscating the lands of rebels. In all, around 450 rebels were executed. Of the leaders, Westmorland escaped abroad, but Northumberland was betrayed by a Scottish clan, eventually being beheaded at York in 1572. The Privy Council demanded Norfolk's execution too, but Elizabeth, out of family loyalty, decided to have him imprisoned at the Tower of London instead. He was released after just nine months, in August 1570.

# The Ridolfi Plot, 1571

Roberto di Ridolfi was a Catholic Italian banker from Florence who lived in London. This plot was again an attempt to restore Catholicism in England. It involved the Queen of Scots, the Pope, Philip II of Spain and the Duke of Norfolk. This time, the plan was far more dangerous. Elizabeth had been excommunicated by the Pope in 1570, so the English Catholics were now free to rebel against their Queen. The plan was simple: for Elizabeth to be assassinated and replaced as monarch by Mary, Queen of Scots. The idea was for around 6000 Spanish troops to land at Harwich in Essex, led by the Duke of Alba.

Their arrival, it was hoped, would prompt a rebellion. Ridolfi optimistically calculated that about half of the English nobles were Catholic and that when they rebelled they would be able to assemble nearly 40,000 men. Once Elizabeth had been murdered, the plan was for Mary to marry the Duke of Norfolk. In prison, Mary was desperate for her freedom, and had lost all hope of Elizabeth helping her to return to either France or Scotland. Norfolk, recently released from prison, was keen to regain power after his disgrace. Both Mary and Norfolk therefore agreed to the plot.

## Consequences

Elizabeth's intelligence network discovered the conspiracy. As Ridolfi was abroad when the plot was discovered, he escaped prosecution. De Spes, the Spanish Ambassador, was expelled from England. Norfolk was arrested and found guilty of treason. Parliament passed a law directed against Mary that declared that anyone making a claim to the throne and knowing of a plan to assassinate the monarch should be removed from the succession. Parliament also pushed for both Norfolk and Mary to be executed. Not for the first or the last time, Elizabeth was indecisive. Norfolk was England's only duke and also her cousin. She had forgiven him once before. She changed her mind three times, but with great reluctance eventually decided to sign Norfolk's DEATH WARRANT. He was beheaded on Tower Hill in June 1572. However, Elizabeth's other cousin, the Queen of Scots, survived the plot. Elizabeth absolutely refused to consider having her executed.

**THINK**

6 Read Source 5. Did Parliament regard Mary as a leader or a mere participant in the plots against Elizabeth?

7 Read Source 6. Why did Elizabeth refuse to have Mary executed in 1572?

> ### SOURCE 5
> Parliament's charges against Mary in May 1572.
>
> *She has wickedly challenged the crown of England. She has sought to withdraw the Duke of Norfolk from his natural obedience. She has stirred the Earls of Northumberland and Westmorland to rebel. She has practised [tried] to procure [start] new rebellion to be raised within this realm. We, your true and obedient subjects, do most humbly beseech Your Majesty to punish and correct all the treasons and wicked attempts of the said Mary.*

> ### SOURCE 6
> Elizabeth's words to her Council in 1572, explaining her position on Mary, Queen of Scots.
>
> *Can I put to death the bird that, to escape the pursuit of the hawk, has fled to my feet for protection? Honour and conscience forbid!*

## The Throckmorton Plot, 1583

In 1583 a plan was hatched for a French Catholic force, backed by Spanish and Papal money, to invade England. Again, the Queen of Scots was central to the scheme. Mary was to be freed from house arrest and there was to be a Catholic uprising involving the Jesuits, seminary priests and English Catholic population. Elizabeth would be captured and, following her murder, Mary was to be installed as Queen. Francis Throckmorton, after whom the plot is named, acted as the intermediary between Mary and the Spanish Ambassador, Bernardino de Mendoza. Before the plan could be put into action, Walsingham discovered what was happening. Throckmorton was placed under surveillance for six months. Once arrested, he was tortured on the rack and made a confession.

Following this plot, the Bond of Association was established, which meant that anybody associated with an assassination plot against Elizabeth would not be allowed to benefit from the Queen's death in any way. Throckmorton himself was convicted of high treason, and was executed in July 1584. De Mendoza was expelled from England, and no more Spanish ambassadors lived in England for the rest of Elizabeth's reign. Once again, a lack of evidence meant that Mary escaped relatively unscathed. However, Walsingham now became determined to find some hard evidence of Mary's treasonous activity so that she could be dealt with once and for all.

## SOURCE 7

From *Mary Queen of Scots* by Antonia Fraser, 1969.

[Mary's] own agreement [to the plot] was entirely in the context of a captive seeking to escape her guards, and may be compared to the actions of a prisoner who is prepared to escape by a certain route, even if it may involve the slaying of a jailer by another hand.

### THINK

8  Why did Mary become involved in the Babington Plot?
9  Why do you think Mary wrote her letters in code?
10  Why did Walsingham set up a conspiracy against Elizabeth?

## SOURCE 8

The cipher code used by Mary, Queen of Scots.

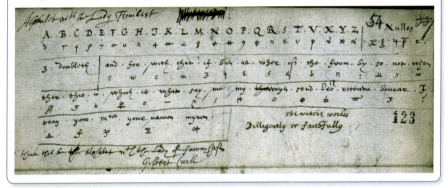

# The Babington Plot, 1586

After the discovery of the Throckmorton Plot, Mary was moved to the ruined Tutbury Castle in Staffordshire and then to a moated manor house called Chartley Hall in late 1585. Here, she was not allowed any visitors and all her letters were checked. Her jailer was a strict Puritan called Amyas Paulet, carefully chosen by Elizabeth because of his hatred of the Catholic faith. Her harsher treatment was not simply a security measure. The idea was to push Mary into another plot. By this time, Mary had become deeply resentful of her situation. She had been imprisoned for almost twenty years. Cut off from the outside world, she had lost her throne, her status, her social life and her son. There seemed little hope of escape, and she was also in failing health, had lost her looks and had become obese.

Mary inevitably became depressed and more resentful of Elizabeth. She began a secret correspondence with the French Ambassador and Sir Anthony Babington. Babington was a Catholic recusant from Derbyshire who had been recruited by a Jesuit priest called John Ballard to help organise a new plot. Letters between the conspirators were written in code and were smuggled in and out of Chartley. By mid-1586, a plot to kill Elizabeth and free Mary had been devised. The plan was to place Mary on the throne and re-establish Catholicism as England's religion, with the help of a Spanish invasion force.

Unknown to Mary, Elizabeth's 'spymaster' Walsingham knew all about the letters. Walsingham had placed a double-agent named Gilbert Gifford inside Chartley. He intercepted the letters, which were then deciphered by Thomas Phelippes, who then sent the details to Walsingham himself. Walsingham allowed the letters to be sent on to their intended recipients in order to allow the plot to unfold in the hope of finally entrapping Mary. It worked. On 17 July 1586, Mary wrote a coded letter approving of the plot and, crucially, consenting to the assassination of Elizabeth. The following month, Babington was arrested, and in September 1586 he and six other conspirators were hung, drawn and quartered.

# The trial and execution of Mary, Queen of Scots

Walsingham now had proof of Mary's guilt. In October, Mary was placed on trial for treason at Fotheringhay Castle in Northamptonshire. She had to manage her own defence, which she did eloquently. She was found guilty. Parliament and the Privy Council insisted that Mary should be executed.

## The death warrant

As in her dealings with Norfolk's treachery fifteen years earlier, Elizabeth was indecisive and angered her advisors with the delays. A letter sent to Elizabeth from Mary was said to have reduced Elizabeth to tears. Eventually, in December 1586, Cecil prepared a death warrant, but Elizabeth refused to sign it. Only in February of the following year, amid rumours of Spanish landings in Wales and Mary's escape, did Elizabeth finally sign the warrant.

However, she said that this was a precautionary measure, giving her secretary instructions not to have the warrant sealed. However, the Council met without Elizabeth's knowledge and took a drastic course of action. The Queen's instructions were ignored. The death warrant was sealed and sent to Fotheringhay. On 8 February 1587, in a bloody and botched execution, Mary, Queen of Scots was beheaded.

## Elizabeth's response

When news of Mary's death was brought to Elizabeth, she reacted with fury. She was appalled at the idea that she had given permission for the murder of a fellow monarch and she appeared to be wracked with guilt over this REGICIDE. She banished Cecil, refusing to see him for six months. Her secretary, William Davison, was imprisoned in the Tower of London. Elizabeth was aware of the dangerous consequences that could result from Mary's death. In killing Mary, Elizabeth had made her into a MARTYR for the Catholic cause. However, English Catholics did not rise up in protest. Appalled at yet another plot against their Queen, they were evidently more loyal to their monarch than Elizabeth thought.

Although the problem of Mary had been permanently removed, her death caused displeasure abroad. England was already at war with Spain, and Mary's death maddened Philip II still further. The King of Scots, unsurprisingly, also protested at his mother's execution and so too did Mary's brother-in-law, the Catholic King of France. However, their protests came to nothing. Elizabeth deflected their anger by claiming her innocence in the whole affair, instead blaming her secretary for not following her instructions about the death warrant. Historians have since questioned whether Elizabeth's outpouring of grief over her cousin's death was genuine. Many have suggested that it was all an act and that Davison was simply a scapegoat used to cover Elizabeth's own ruthlessness in getting rid of Mary once and for all.

**THINK**

11 How do Elizabeth's views differ from Mary's according to Sources 9 and 10?
12 In Source 11, what does Fraser suggest about Mary's trial?
13 Read Source 12. Why do you think secretary Davison and the Council acted in the way they did?
14 Read Source 13. How do you think people would have reacted to hearing the story of Mary's execution?
15 How convincing is Source 14 about Elizabeth's reaction to Mary's death?

### SOURCE 9
Mary's words spoken to her jailer, Sir Amyas Paulet, in October 1586.

*'As a sinner I am truly conscious of having often offended my Creator and I beg Him to forgive me, but as a Queen and Sovereign, I am aware of no fault or offence for which I have to render account to anyone here below.'*

### SOURCE 10
Elizabeth's response to Mary's protests.

*'You have in various ways and manners attempted to take my life and to bring my kingdom to destruction by bloodshed.'*

### SOURCE 11
From *Mary Queen of Scots* by Antonia Fraser, 1969.

*How, indeed, could it ever be legal for Mary as sovereign, the Queen of a foreign country, to be tried for treason, when she was in no sense one of Elizabeth's subjects?*

### SOURCE 12
From *Tudor England* by John Guy (1988).

*[Davison] had [the warrant] sealed at once, and, at a crisis meeting of the eleven councillors... it was decided to despatch the warrant and not to inform the Queen 'before the execution were past'.*

### SOURCE 13
From *The History of Britain Vol. 1* by Simon Schama, 2000.

*And when the executioner went to perform his obligatory duty of holding up the head and calling out 'God Save the Queen', he made the mistake of grasping it by the mass of auburn curls. It was, of course, a wig. To general horror, Mary's skull, covered only with a mat of grey stubble, fell from the hair and rolled across the floor like a bowling ball.*

### SOURCE 14
From a letter written by Elizabeth to Mary's son, James VI of Scots, after the execution.

*My dearest Brother, I would to God thou knowest (but not that thou feltest) the incomparable grief my mind is perplexed with upon this lamentable accident, which is happened contrary to my meaning and intention.*

### SOURCE 15
From *England under the Tudors* by G.R. Elton (1955).

*The martyrdom of the Queen of Scots remains a stain on the record of Elizabeth's reign.*

## PRACTICE QUESTIONS

1 Explain what was important about Mary, Queen of Scots' presence in England between 1568 and 1587.
2 Write an account of the ways Roman Catholics plotted to remove Elizabeth from the throne.

## FOCUS TASK B

### The impact of Mary Queen of Scots on Elizabethan England

You have been making notes about the life of Mary, Queen of Scots. Use your notes to tackle the following questions:

1 Was Mary guilty of treason?
2 Did Elizabeth make a mistake in having Mary executed?
3 Write an obituary for Mary, Queen of Scots showing your understanding of her life and her impact on Elizabethan England. The obituary is to appear in a government publication in England, so it should be written in a one-sided manner. The whole piece should aim to justify Mary's death and defend Elizabeth's actions.

## TIP

Make sure you can explain various reasons why Mary, Queen of Scots was executed in 1587.

## KEYWORDS

Make sure you know what various words mean and are able to use them confidently in your own writing. See the glossary on page 94 for definitions.
- Abdicate
- Ambassador
- Death warrant
- House arrest
- Martyr
- Regicide

## TOPIC SUMMARY

### Mary, Queen of Scots

- Mary, Queen of Scots was half-French, Catholic and Elizabeth's cousin.
- Mary was a potential heir to the English throne.
- Mary was considered by some Catholics to be the rightful Queen of England.
- After she fled Scotland, Mary was held a prisoner in England for nineteen years in remote locations.
- Mary was involved in four Catholic plots against Elizabeth.
- Walsingham eventually entrapped Mary in the Babington Plot.
- Mary was tried for treason and was executed in February 1587.
- Elizabeth's instructions regarding Mary's death warrant were ignored by her Councillors.

# 3.3 Conflict with Spain

## FOCUS

By the mid-1580s, tension between England and Spain erupted into open war. Then, in 1588, a huge fleet of Spanish ships was launched to attack England. This Catholic 'crusade' was the most serious danger posed to English national security during the entire Tudor period, but the ARMADA was miraculously defeated. In topic 3.3 you will:

● understand why England and Spain went to war
● examine the key events of the Spanish Armada
● discover why the Spanish Armada failed.

## THINK

1 Study Source 1 carefully. Which side (England or Spain) appears to be the strongest at this stage in the conflict?

## FOCUS TASK A

### The Spanish Armada

As you study section 1 draw up a mind map to summarise the key elements of the story of the Spanish Armada. Start with branches for:

● The causes of conflict
● The Spanish invasion plan
● The leaders
● Resources
● The key events

● The technology and tactics
● The role of the weather
● The consequences for
  – England
  – Spain.

## SOURCE 1

A drawing of the Spanish Armada in the English Channel. The Spanish fleet, in crescent formation, is on the right. The English ships are on the left. In the foreground some English ships are attacking a Spanish ship.

# Causes of the conflict with Spain
## Religious differences

Ever since Elizabeth's accession, relations between England and Spain had been tense. An uneasy peace existed between the two nations. The Spanish King had been Bloody Mary's husband. Keen to keep his influence, he had proposed marriage to his former sister-in-law in 1559. Elizabeth's rejection had angered him. Philip also hated Elizabeth's Protestant religious settlement. As a devout Catholic, Philip saw Elizabeth as a HERETIC who should not be on the throne. Conquering England in order to restore Catholicism was, to him, a just cause.

## Rebellion in the Netherlands

Poor Anglo-Spanish relations were further complicated by events in the Spanish-ruled Netherlands. Philip had the difficult task of ruling very different territories that were hundreds of miles apart. Unlike in Spain, most people in the Netherlands were Protestant and they disliked the firm hand of Catholic rule. Civil war broke out in 1566 and the Duke of Alba was sent by Philip, along with 10,000 troops, to deal with the rebels in a brutal manner. This brutality increased hatred of Spain in England. Aside from religious matters, Elizabeth also had a strong interest in events in the Netherlands because the rebellion affected England. The English economy relied on the cloth trade based at Antwerp. Various trade restrictions were brought in which disrupted English business.

It was in England's interests for the rebellion to be resolved, and for the Protestants to overthrow Spanish rule. Spain was the richest and most powerful European power. Elizabeth did not want the Netherlands – on England's doorstep, just the other side of the English Channel – to be ruled over by a hostile Catholic power. However, if Elizabeth was too open in her support of the Dutch Protestants, she would provoke a war with Philip that England could not afford. As a solution to this problem, the so-called 'Peace Party' on the Privy Council gave indirect help to the rebels. It was a difficult balancing act. Unofficially, England helped the Protestant cause by allowing rebel ships to stay in English ports and by allowing English pirates to attack and disrupt Spanish supply lines to the Netherlands. From 1581, Elizabeth also sent the rebels funds to help their fight against Spanish rule.

### THINK

2  Why might the Spanish have wanted to invade England in 1588?
3  Why would Elizabeth want Dutch rebels to succeed in overthrowing Spanish rule in the Netherlands?

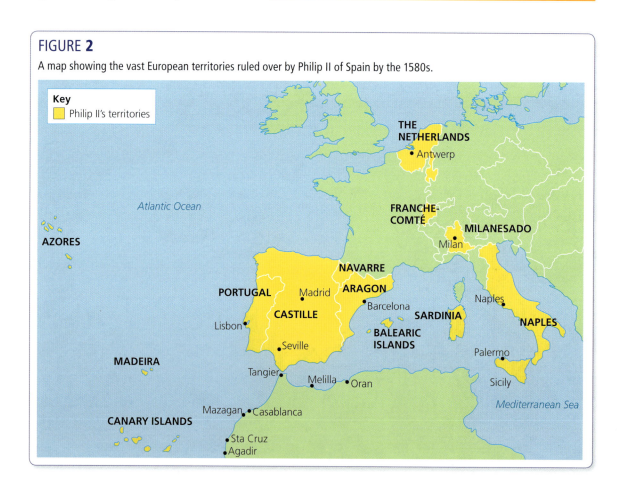

**FIGURE 2**

A map showing the vast European territories ruled over by Philip II of Spain by the 1580s.

**SOURCE 3**

A painting about the situation in the Netherlands. The cow represents the Netherlands. Philip II is shown riding on the back of the cow, as he was a burden on the country. The Spanish commander is shown to be milking the cow, representing Spanish exploitation. Elizabeth I, meanwhile, is shown to be feeding the cow, to symbolise the aid she gave to the rebellion in terms of troops and money.

## Privateers, plots and persecution

Other factors increased Anglo-Spanish tensions. Attacks on Spanish treasure ships by English privateers such as Francis Drake angered the Spanish, as did Elizabeth's support for French HUGUENOTS. Encouraged by the Pope, Philip had also been plotting against Elizabeth. The Spanish Ambassadors in England had been involved in plots surrounding Mary, Queen of Scots which made the English more suspicious of the Spanish. Meanwhile, Elizabeth's reaction to the plots was to persecute the English Catholics. This made Philip more determined that something must be done about England.

## Why did tension turn to war?

- Courtiers, including Walsingham and Dudley, called for military action. Both sides made formal alliances. Spain signed the Treaty of Joinville with the French in 1584, boosting Spanish confidence and raising English fears of a possible Catholic invasion.
- Meanwhile, the Protestant cause in the Netherlands was struggling. The Spanish governor, the Duke of Parma, was successfully crushing the rebellion and the rebel leader William 'the Silent' was assassinated. This pushed the English into making formal the unofficial help they had already provided. In 1585, the Treaty of Nonsuch was signed between England and the Dutch rebels. England agreed to send 7000 troops – under Dudley's command – to support the rebellion in the Netherlands. After years of tension and unofficial conflict, England and Spain were formally at war.
- Philip had already begun to seriously contemplate an invasion of England when, in 1587, Mary, Queen of Scots was executed. Catholic Europe was outraged at what it saw as an unjustified murder. For Philip, this was the final straw. The time had come for the so-called 'Enterprise of England'.

### The Duke of Parma

- The nephew of Philip II.
- Governor of the Spanish Netherlands, 1578–92.
- In charge of stopping the Protestant revolt.
- An expert military leader.
- Wanted to use his large army to conquer England.
- The Armada was to pick up his troops, but poor communication prevented this.

### The Duke of Medina Sidonia

- One of the wealthiest Spanish noblemen.
- Chosen to lead the Armada after Philip's first choice died.
- Lacking in self-confidence, tried to turn down the position offered.
- Doubted the chances of the Armada's success.
- A capable soldier, but he had no experience of fighting at sea.
- Showed little initiative, and his incompetence was a significant factor in the Armada's failure.
- One of the few to survive the Armada and make it back to Spain.

### SOURCE 4

An extract from a letter written by the Duke of Medina Sidonia to Philip II.

*I wish I possessed the talents and strength necessary to it. But Sir, I have not the health for the sea. I soon become seasick. It would not be right for a person like myself, possessing no experience of seafaring or war, to take charge of it.*

### SOURCE 5

From *The Spanish Armada* by C. Martin and G. Parker (1988).

*For Medina Sidonia to have expected rapid and reliable communications between himself and Parma once he had put to sea reveals a profound misunderstanding of the logistical limitations of his position.*

### THINK

4  Read the text and Sources 4 and 5. What was the major flaw in Philip's plan?

# Spanish plans for invasion

Plans for a Spanish invasion of England were delayed for more than a year by Francis Drake's raid on Spanish ships at Cádiz, which destroyed much of the Spanish fleet and their supplies. This did not stop Philip. He prepared a huge fleet of 130 ships armed with 2500 guns. The plan was for the Armada to sail up the English Channel in order to meet up with the Spanish army in the Netherlands. This army, numbering about 30,000 men, was under the command of the brilliant Duke of Parma. Once the troops had been picked up, the plan was for the ships to cross the Channel and capture ports on the south coast. Once they had landed, the invasion force would march on London. The English Catholics were also expected to rise up in rebellion in support of the Spanish, forcing Elizabeth off the throne.

# Leadership of the two sides

Philip had appointed the Duke of Medina Sidonia to lead the Armada. A senior Spanish nobleman, he was chosen more because of his rank than his ability. He was actually a very poor choice, as he had no experience of being at sea. In contrast, the English fleet was expertly led by the Queen's cousin, Lord Howard, and several other men. Howard was Lord High Admiral and was ably assisted by Sir Francis Drake as his second-in-command. The latter, hated by the Spanish, was very experienced at hit-and-run tactics, as were the two other main English commanders involved, John Hawkins and Martin Frobisher.

# Resources of the two sides

Philip had huge resources at his disposal. Elizabeth was, in comparison, weak. She did not have a full-time army, but had put plans in place by ordering every county to provide soldiers. About 20,000 were gathered but, unlike Philip's professional army, they had little training or equipment. As she did not know where the Spanish would land, Elizabeth had to spread her men along the coast. The main armies were placed in the North of England, in Kent and at Tilbury, in Essex. On paper, Elizabeth was also relatively weak at sea. There were just 34 battleships in the English navy. However, private individuals and trading companies were ordered to make their ships available and these were quickly prepared for war. In this way, about 200 ships were ready for use.

# The launch of the Armada

With the plan in place, the Armada left Lisbon in May 1588, but early events did not suggest that things would go well. The fleet quickly ran into storms, losing supplies, and forcing the ships back for repairs. They set sail again, this time entering the English Channel successfully in a defensive crescent formation. The slower unarmed galleons and store-ships were well protected in the middle and the faster, heavily armed ships sailed on the outside.

Philip's plan was to pick up troops in the Netherlands, so the Armada had to pass by the entire English coast. Given the size of the Armada, this could not go unnoticed. The English first spotted the Spanish on 19 July, off Lizard Point in Cornwall. A system of BEACONS that had been built across the south coast were lit to send news of the Armada's arrival to London. Church bells were also rung out in warning.

As the Spanish sailed up the Channel, they were followed by the English fleet. There were a few encounters, but the Armada successfully maintained its crescent formation and only three Spanish ships were lost. However, the Armada was in trouble. A key part of Philip's plan relied on close communication between Medina Sidonia at sea and Parma in the Netherlands, but this was of course impossible. Indeed, the whole mission was poorly planned.

# Ship design

The English explorer and naval commander Hawkins had spent years making improvements to the design of English ships. They were now lighter, faster and more manoeuvrable than those in the Spanish fleet, which consisted of large, slow galleons. The English were also careful to keep their distance from the Spanish, using light and accurate long-range guns called CULVERINS to attack while at a safe distance. This was a good tactical move, frustrating the Spanish by making it impossible for them to employ their usual naval tactics. The Spanish relied on getting close to the enemy, using short-range guns to overcome their adversaries and then employing grappling hooks in order to board enemy ships and take them over.

# Fireships

With the winds rising sharply, the Armada anchored at Calais. The cunning Drake then pulled a master stroke. On the night of 28 July, eight old English ships were filled with tar and oil and set on fire. These fireships were then allowed to drift into the anchored Spanish fleet. Although no Spanish ships actually burnt, the approaching fireships terrified the Spaniards. The crews panicked and cut their anchor ropes, fleeing out to sea. Some crashed into each other and others ran aground. Crucially, in the panic the Spanish ships were scattered by the wind and were blown towards dangerous sandbanks off the coast of the Netherlands. The English had succeeded in breaking the tight crescent formation that the Spanish had maintained up to this point.

> ## SOURCE 7
>
> An extract from the Duke of Medina Sidonia's report to King Philip.
>
> *There were eight vessels with sails set, which were drifting with the current directly towards our flagship and the rest of the Armada, all of them burning with great fury. When I saw them approaching, fearing that they might contain fire machines or mines, I ordered the flagship to let go the cables, the rest of the Armada receiving similar orders, with an indication that when the fires had passed they were to return to the same positions again. The current was so strong that most of the ships of the Armada were carried towards Dunkirk.*

# Gravelines and Tilbury

The next day, the two fleets engaged in combat at the Battle of Gravelines, off the coast of Flanders. The English now had the advantage. They had broken the Spanish formation and forced the Armada to sail into the wind. In addition, the manoeuvrable English ships were now a tactical advantage. The Spanish were provoked into firing at the English while they were out of range. Their guns were poorly designed and took up so much deck space that they proved impossible to reload after firing just once. The English culverins, in contrast, could be quickly reloaded and now battered the Spanish fleet by firing repeated BROADSIDES. They aimed low, hitting the enemy ships below the waterline. The English did not lose a single ship. The battle was a disaster for the Spanish. About a thousand Spanish lives were lost. They lost five ships and many more were badly damaged. However, even at this point there were still considerable fears that Parma might still attempt an invasion. Typically melodramatic, Elizabeth visited her troops at Tilbury on horseback and clad in armour. There, in one of her most famous actions as Queen, Elizabeth made a rousing speech (Source 8).

> ## SOURCE 6
>
> A traditional story about Sir Francis Drake's reaction when told the Armada had been sighted.
>
> *The English commanders were playing bowls in Plymouth when they heard that the Armada had been sighted. Drake said 'There is time to finish the game and beat the Spaniards too.' They finished the game before heading for their ships.*

> ## SOURCE 8
>
> An extract from Elizabeth's speech to her troops at Tilbury in Essex.
>
> *I am resolved in the midst and heat of battle to live and die among you all. I know that I have the body of a weak and feeble woman, but I have the heart and stomach of a King, and of a King of England too, and think foul scorn that Parma or Spain, or any other Prince of Europe should dare to invade the borders of my realm.*

## THINK

5 Why was the English use of fireships such a good strategy?
6 Why did the Spanish lose the Battle of Gravelines?
7 Why did Elizabeth make the speech in Source 8?

## FACTFILE

### The Spanish Armada

- The Armada was first spotted at Lizard Point in Cornwall, the most southerly point of the British mainland.

- A chain of beacons had been constructed along the south coast on high ground to alert London of a coming invasion. Some still survive, such as the beacon above the village of Culmstock in Devon.

- The Solent is the narrow channel of water separating the Isle of Wight from the English mainland. Medina Sidonia wanted to establish a temporary base in these calm and protected waters in order to wait for news from Parma and his army, but the English prevented this from happening.

- The English pushed the Armada towards the Owers, a group of dangerous ledges and rocks just south of Selsey. This forced the Armada away from the coast and into open sea, giving them no choice but to head for Calais, without having any word from Parma.

- Once the Armada reached Calais, fireships were used by the English. This scattered the Spanish crescent formation and they were then defeated in the Battle of Gravelines. The Spanish were then chased by the English as far north as the Firth of Forth in Scotland.

- Tilbury is in Essex on the north bank of the River Thames. It was the location of a fort that had been built by Henry VIII in 1539. It was built to defend London from attack from the sea. It was reinforced in the summer of 1588 with two concentric earthwork ramparts with ditches and a palisade. Elizabeth gave a rousing speech to her 4000 troops who were encamped near to the fort on 8 August. Even though the Armada had been chased as far as Scotland by this point, it was still feared that Parma might invade.

- On their journey home, the Spanish were equipped with poor maps and were not aware of the effect of the Gulf Stream in the North Atlantic. Thinking they had sailed much further west of the British Isles than they actually had, they turned south much too early. Gales and strong westerly winds then drove many of their ships on to rocks off the north and west coast of Ireland.

## THINK

8 How does a study of the places mentioned in the Factfile above help you to understand the defeat of the Spanish Armada?

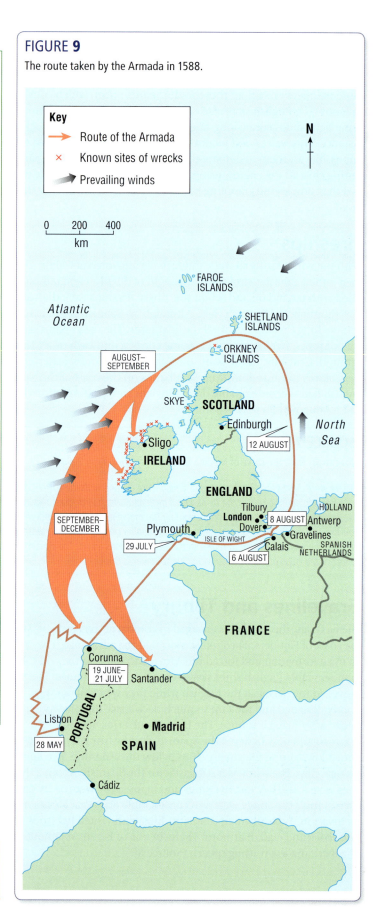

### FIGURE 9

The route taken by the Armada in 1588.

# Defeat of the Armada

Elizabeth need not have worried. There would be no invasion. Medina Sidonia knew they were beaten. With God's 'Protestant wind' blowing from the south west, the damaged Spanish fleet was blown into gales in the North Sea. The change in wind direction meant that there was now no chance of the Armada meeting up with Parma's troops in the Netherlands. The fleet had no choice but to head home. With the English Channel manned by the English fleet, the only way back to Spain was to sail north. The Armada was chased by the English as far as the Scottish border. The English then turned back. In September, the beleaguered Spanish fleet sailed around the coast of Scotland and Ireland. They were battered by storms, running short of supplies, and lacked any accurate maps of these areas. Many of the sailors fell ill and many vessels were shipwrecked. Of Philip's mighty fleet, just 60 ships had made it back to Spain by the end of the year. An estimated 20,000 Spaniards had been killed. For the Spanish, the Armada had been an epic military failure, and a huge waste of human life and resources.

**THINK**

9   Why did the English defeat the Armada? List the reasons and then decide the most important, in your opinion.

10  Why did the Armada take such a long route home (see Figure 9)?

> ## SOURCE 10
>
> A report written by a Spanish general on the Armada's defeat.
>
> *We found that many of the enemy's ships held great advantages over us in combat, both in the design, and in their guns, gunners and crews who could do with us as they wished.*

> ## SOURCE 11
>
> From *The Spanish Armada* by Felipe Fernandez-Armesto (1989).
>
> *Good weather... was essential for Spanish success. It was the least of the miracles they expected from God.*

# Aftermath of Spain's defeat

Philip was bitterly disappointed at his humiliating defeat. There were great celebrations in England, and the victory had enormous propaganda value for Elizabeth. National pride was boosted. England's independence had been safeguarded and Protestantism had been preserved. The important role played by the wind in England's victory was of course taken as a sure sign of God's approval of Protestantism. The victory also paved the way for England to establish itself as a major naval power. The English commanders had been creative in the tactics they had used. In particular, they had shown the importance of guns in sea battles, which had a lasting impact on naval tactics.

The Anglo-Spanish War dragged on long after the dramatic events of 1588. The English launched an unsuccessful counter-Armada against Spain in 1589, and Philip launched two further Armadas in 1596 and 1597, but both were driven back by storms. Elizabeth carried on offering help to the Dutch rebels and the English continued to attack Spanish treasure ships and ports. Philip continued to try to stir up trouble among Elizabeth's Catholic subjects, even aiding a rebellion in Ireland. The war put huge strain on the struggling English economy, causing inflation and hardship for the poor. Ultimately, the war lasted beyond the deaths of both Philip and Elizabeth, only ending in 1604. Neither side really won.

> ## SOURCE 12
>
> An English medal commemorating the Armada. Its inscription reads 'He blew with His winds, and they were scattered.'
>
>
>

> ## SOURCE 13
>
> From *Elizabeth I* by Christopher Haigh (1988).
>
> *The defeat of the Spanish Armada in 1588 solved nothing. There was still a successful Spanish army in the Netherlands, still Spanish support for French Catholics against the Huguenots, and still a risk of Spanish invasions.*

**THINK**

11  What are the messages conveyed by the painting in Source 14?
12  Was the significance of the Armada's defeat exaggerated by English propaganda?

**SOURCE 14**

'The Armada Portrait' of Elizabeth was painted to celebrate the events of 1588.

**PRACTICE QUESTIONS**

1  Explain the reasons why England was at war with Spain in the 1580s.
2  Write an account of the defeat of the Spanish Armada in 1588.

**FOCUS TASK B**

**Why was the Armada defeated?**

Now you've completed your mind map of the key elements of the Spanish Armada:

1  Write down three pieces of evidence for each of the following themes that explain the Armada's defeat.
   •  Spanish weaknesses       •  English strengths       •  Luck
2  Of the three themes above, explain which one you think was the most important cause of the Spanish defeat.
3  You have been commissioned by a TV production company to write a script about the Spanish Armada focusing on the reasons for their defeat. It is only 30 minutes long. In your script you should include:
   •  Why Philip attached England
   •  Weaknesses in Spanish plans
   •  Weaknesses in Spanish leadership
   •  Differences between British and Spanish ships
   •  The role of the weather
   •  English tactics (such as the fireships)
   •  Key event: The Battle of Gravelines
   •  Why victory was important for Elizabeth and England

**TIP**

Make sure you can explain several reasons why England and Spain went to war and also why the Spanish Armada was defeated.

**TOPIC SUMMARY**

**Conflict with Spain**

●  Tensions between England and Spain, and Philip and Elizabeth, existed for years before they officially went to war.
●  A rebellion in the Netherlands threatened Spanish power and disrupted English trade.
●  Spain had been involved in Mary, Queen of Scots' Catholic plots against Elizabeth.
●  The most famous event of the conflict was the Spanish Armada of 1588, which aimed to invade and conquer England.
●  The Armada was defeated due to Spanish mistakes, the tactical skill of the English and the weather.
●  The Spanish defeat boosted English national pride and was a great propaganda victory for Elizabeth.

**KEYWORDS**

Make sure you know what these words mean and are able to use them confidently in your own writing. See the glossary on page 94 for definitions.
●  Armada
●  Beacon
●  Broadside
●  Culverins
●  Huguenot

# REVIEW of Chapter 3

## Trouble at home and abroad

Here is another opportunity to review your learning using another FOUR practice questions.

**Question 1** will be on interpretations. You need to use your knowledge to explain how convincing an interpretation is. The interpretation could be a picture or a written source. For example:

> ### INTERPRETATION C
>
> An interpretation of the Spanish fleet anchored at Calais being attacked by an English fireship.
>
>

> 1. How convincing is Interpretation C about the reasons for the defeat of the Spanish Armada?
>
> Explain your answer using Interpretation C and your contextual knowledge. (8 marks)

For this question, you need to describe what you can see and then use detailed knowledge to support and contradict what the source suggests about the defeat of the Spanish Armada.

**Question 2** will ask you to explain the significance or importance of something. For example:

> 2. Explain what was important about the Spanish Netherlands during the Elizabethan period. (8 marks)

There are many things you could cover but you need to focus on the ones that show the importance of the issue not on incidental details.

> Consider how the source is convincing in the reasons it suggests for the Armada's defeat. Think about:
> - Who decided to use fireships? Why?
> - How were the Spanish affected by the fireships?
> - How was the design of the Spanish ships a hindrance?
>
> Consider how the source is not convincing. Think about:
> - Does it exaggerate any features of the incident of the role played by this fireship in the Armada's defeat?
> - How many fireships were actually used?
> - How effective were the Spanish guns?
>
> Look back at topic 3.3 to see how you could expand on these points.

> Which of the following do you think you should spend most time on?
> - The importance of Antwerp to English trade
> - The location of the Spanish Netherlands in Europe
> - The Protestant rebellion
> - Elizabeth's aid for the Dutch rebels
> - Spain's response to English interference
>
> Look back at topic 3.3 to see how you could expand on your chosen points.

You could include:
- Mary's background
- Elizabeth's imprisonment of Mary
- Catholic plots involving Mary
- Mary's execution and its consequences

Look back at topic 3.2 to see if you can write a paragraph on one or more of these points.

Read the information below, and use topic 3.1 to map out the key points of your possible answer under five headings:
- How did Elizabeth persecute Catholics?
- Why did Elizabeth persecute Catholics?
- What measures did Catholics take to keep Catholicism strong? Think about plots, missionaries and safe houses.
- How are these measures represented at Harvington?
- How typical of Elizabethan manor houses was Harvington?

Then if you are really brave have a go at writing a full essay.

**Question 3** asks you to write an account. It is still not 'everything you know'. You are selecting from your knowledge those things that are most relevant to answer the question. For example:

> 3. Write an account of the ways in which Mary, Queen of Scots affected Elizabethan England. (8 marks)

For this question you need to cover a range of events with enough detail to show you understand the different effects Mary, Queen of Scots had on Elizabethan England. You need to write your answer in the form of a coherent narrative.

**Question 4** is on the historic environment – an actual site chosen by the exam board that you will have studied, in depth. You use your knowledge of the site, and your wider knowledge of Elizabethan England to write an essay that evaluates a statement.

There will be so much you could say about the site that you have to be selective. The statement in the question provides the focus for you to develop a clear, coherent and relevant argument.

The nominated site changes every year. However, you can practise with any site. So below you will find a Factfile of information about a very interesting Tudor building, Harvington Hall, which is famous for its priest holes.

> 4. 'The main change that some Elizabethan manor houses demonstrated was their owners' determination to support Catholicism.' How far does a study of Harvington Hall support this statement? (16 marks)

The key thing to remember about question 4 is that it is inviting you to reach a judgement – agreeing or disagreeing with the statement and using the site to support your answer.

## FACTFILE

### Harvington Hall

- Harvington Hall is an Elizabethan manor house in Worcestershire. It is in the countryside between Bromsgrove and Kidderminster. Built on a moated site of an earlier medieval house, Harvington Hall was built by Humphrey Pakington in the 1580s. Pakington was a member of the gentry, a devout Catholic and a recusant.
- Protestantism was strongest in the South East of England. Many disliked Elizabeth's religious settlement. From the 1570s, Catholics faced increasing government persecution and various anti-Catholic laws were passed. Seminary priests and Jesuits were smuggled into the country to keep Catholicism alive. Recusants were fined increasingly large amounts of money for

not attending the Anglican Church. Lands were confiscated. Hearing the Mass was illegal and Catholic priests were considered guilty of treason. Many Catholics were executed.
- A network of 'safe houses' for Catholics was set up. Suspected houses were raided by pursuivants. Those found to be sheltering priests faced severe punishments.
- Harvington is famous for its many ingenious priest holes. There are seven in total. Many of Harvington's priest holes were made by the renowned carpenter and Jesuit, Nicholas Owen. They are so good that no priest was ever discovered at Harvington.
- One of the priest holes, in the library, was only accidentally discovered in Victorian times. It was concealed behind a pivoted timber beam in the wall panelling. In another room, a false fireplace, blackened for effect, led to a hiding place in the attic above. The most sophisticated priest hole is located under the staircase. Two steps are linked by a hinge so they can be lifted. Via a secret panel at the back of the concealed chamber there is a second chamber, almost impossible to find.
- The house also had a hidden chapel where Mass could be held. Floorboards in the corner of the chapel can be raised so that the paraphernalia used in the Mass could be hidden during a raid on the house.

# Conclusion

The long reign of 'Good Queen Bess' brought political stability, a 'Golden Age' of culture, and a spectacular victory over the Spanish Armada. The government propaganda machine carefully crafted an image of Elizabeth that captured the attention of many at the time and which has shaped historians' opinions of her ever since. Above all, she proved all her doubters wrong. Elizabeth showed that women could rule just as well as men. However, as the sixteenth century drew to its close 'Gloriana' became increasingly frail. Elizabeth's physical decline mirrored a decline in England's fortunes in her last years. England was locked in a long and pointless war with Spain. Religious persecution was common. Inflation was high. Poverty and disease were widespread. The harvest repeatedly failed.

As her closest friends and advisors died one by one, Elizabeth became a lonely and isolated figure. She seemed to lose touch with her people and her grip on government. The Queen became increasingly argumentative, lost her appetite and suffered from insomnia. The final blow was the death of her close friend and cousin, the Countess of Nottingham, in February 1603. Elizabeth sank into a deep depression. Even as she lay dying, the Queen refused to name her successor. She finally died in her sleep on 24 March 1603, aged 69, after a reign of over 44 years. Elizabeth was buried four days later in Westminster Abbey. It was the end of an era, for it was not just Elizabeth who had died. The passing of the 'Virgin Queen' also marked the death of the Tudor dynasty and the end of the Tudor age.

**THINK**

1 How do you think the English people would have reacted to news of the Queen's death?

2 How and why do the interpretations of Elizabeth in Sources 1 and 3 differ?

## SOURCE 1

An extract from a history of Elizabeth's reign written by William Camden in 1615.

*Those golden years. She maintained the dignity of England all her lifetime with peace, prosperity and glory. For never was a prince more beloved, obeyed or more admired abroad.*

## SOURCE 2

Elizabeth's funeral procession.

**FOCUS TASK**

Review your learning by completing the following:

1 Draw a timeline of the key events in Elizabeth's life and reign. Then colour-code it according to the following themes: government, succession, religion, society, culture, trade and foreign affairs.

2 Use your timeline to draw up a table summarising the major successes and failures of Elizabeth and her reign. If possible, try to link the items on both sides of the table.

3 Should Elizabeth be called 'Elizabeth the Great'? Use your timeline and table to write a judgement summing up your overall opinion of Elizabeth. Ensure you justify your opinions by supporting them with evidence.

## SOURCE 3

From *Elizabeth I* by Christopher Haigh (1988).

*Elizabeth died unloved and it was partly her own fault. She ended her days as an irascible [bad-tempered] old woman, presiding over war and failure abroad and poverty and factionalism [divisions] at home. Her reign had been thirty years of illusions, followed by fifteen of disillusion. The English never loved the real Elizabeth, they loved the image she created.*

# ASSESSMENT FOCUS

## Elizabethan England c1568–1603

### How the British Depth Studies will be assessed

There will be four questions which will test three of the assessment objectives:

- AO1 – knowledge and understanding
- AO2 – explanation and analysis
- AO4 – interpretations

The British Depth Studies will be examined in Paper 2. All four British Depth Studies will be on the same paper so make sure you pick the right one! The questions could be on any part of the content so you should aim to revise it all.

| Question | Type | Marks | | | | |
|---|---|---|---|---|---|---|
| | | AO1 | AO2 | AO3 | AO4 | Total marks |
| 1 | How convincing…? How far do you agree? | | | | 8 | 8 |
| 2 | Explain | 4 | 4 | | | 8 |
| 3 | Write an account | 4 | 4 | | | 8 |
| 4 | Essay linked to historical site | 8 | 8 | | 4 | 16 |

When you are revising it is sometimes a good idea to attempt an exam question before you re-read the relevant section in the textbook. You don't need to write the answer in full *before* you re-read the text. You could just plan an answer, or draw up a spider diagram or list of ideas. The important thing is to try very hard to remember what you can before you check what you have done. Once you have re-read the relevant section of the textbook then you should try to write a full answer.

### The exam questions

#### Question 1

Question 1 will focus on interpretations. You will be given one visual or written interpretation of some aspect of the specification content, for example about a named individual, a battle or a development. You will be asked to comment on how convincing the interpretation is. For example:

---

**INTERPRETATION A**

From a book by Christopher Haigh (1988)

*Elizabeth adopted a tone of condescending superiority towards her Parliaments, confident that if she explained things often enough and slowly enough, the little boys would understand. For Elizabeth, parliamentarians were little boys – sometimes unruly and usually a nuisance, and always a waste of an intelligent woman's time. Queen Elizabeth did not like Parliaments and it showed.*

---

This answer addresses some really important points, covering things that make the interpretation convincing and less convincing.

The answer is effective but there is room for improvement. It chooses some good examples to demonstrate how the source is convincing. However, it does not give any examples to support its comments on how the source is unconvincing.

1. How convincing is Interpretation A about Elizabeth's relationship with Parliament? Explain your answer using Interpretation A and your contextual knowledge. (8 marks)

*On the one hand, this interpretation is convincing about Elizabeth's feelings of 'superiority' and her negative attitude towards Parliament. For instance, they pressured her to marry so often that she eventually lost her temper and forbade them from discussing the marriage issue again. She also limited their freedom of speech on religious matters and imprisoned Puritan MPs such as Peter Wentworth when they went too far. She aimed to influence their decisions, often attending Parliament in person in order to bully and charm them into doing what she wanted. However, the interpretation underplays how much Elizabeth actually relied on Parliament to run the country and it exaggerates how powerful Elizabeth really was.*

**OVER TO YOU**

Write two more sentences about whether Elizabeth had to rely heavily on Parliament and whether she lost control over it during her reign.

## Question 2

Question 2 will ask you to explain some feature, development or change. It might be about:

- a change you have studied
- the causes or consequences of an event
- the importance of some key features or characteristics of a period.

For example:

> 2. Explain what was important about Mary, Queen of Scots during the Elizabethan period. (8 marks)

There is more to this than knowledge. You should aim to select the knowledge that is relevant to the question, write in clear language and include plenty of relevant detail to support your answer. The focus of the question is on the importance of Mary, so the points you make and the knowledge that you use to support those points should focus on her impact on England and on Elizabeth. Why was she such a worry to Elizabeth that in the end Mary was executed?

*Mary, Queen of Scots made her cousin Elizabeth feel insecure and she caused instability. After fleeing Scotland in disgrace, Mary sought refuge in England. However, Elizabeth saw her as a dangerous rival and kept her imprisoned in remote locations for nineteen years. A number of plots centred around Mary because she was a Catholic. The Catholics saw Mary as an alternative monarch to Elizabeth. The Northern Rebellion involved a plan to free Mary from captivity and marry her to the leading English nobleman, the Duke of Norfolk. Later, the Ridolfi Plot and Throckmorton Plot also planned to free Mary and to overthrow Elizabeth.*

*Eventually, Mary was put on trial and found guilty of treason for her involvement in the Babington Plot. She had written coded letters, supporting a conspiracy to have Elizabeth assassinated and herself placed on the throne. The letters had been intercepted by Elizabeth's spymaster, Sir Francis Walsingham. The proof of Mary's guilt led to her execution in February 1587.*

*Her execution was very important, as it angered Catholics across Europe, particularly King Philip II of Spain. Mary was considered a Catholic martyr and Elizabeth was accused of regicide. Indeed, Elizabeth herself went into a deep depression due to the guilt she felt over Mary's death and she had her secretary imprisoned for his part in dispatching the death warrant.*

This answer seems like a good one, because it covers a number of consequences of Mary's presence in Elizabethan England. It details Mary's involvement in various Catholic plots against Elizabeth, her eventual execution, and the impact this had on Elizabeth's security and reputation.

However, to do really well you should refer to wider political and religious events during Elizabeth's reign and how they connect to the story of Mary, Queen of Scots. For example:

- Why did Elizabeth's decision to remain unmarried make Mary more of a threat?
- Why did Catholics not like Elizabeth or her religious settlement?
- What impact did Elizabeth's excommunication by the Pope have on events?
- How is Mary's execution linked to the Spanish Armada?

### OVER TO YOU

Choose one of these points and write another paragraph.

## Question 3

Question 3 asks you to write a narrative account of some change or development from the period. For example:

> 3. Write an account of the ways in which conflict with Spain affected Elizabethan England. (8 marks)

The big difference between Questions 2 and 3 is that in Question 3 you are trying to write an orderly account of the changes that happened, and the effects on Elizabethan England over time, as a result of the issue mentioned in the question. This is still not 'everything you know' about a topic. You still need to select knowledge carefully that shows you understand England's conflict with Spain and its effects on England.

This is an effective answer because it demonstrates accurate factual knowledge about Anglo-Spanish relations and about the Spanish Armada, its most significant episode.

It is written in a narrative style and shows chronological understanding. It shows an awareness of the key short-term consequences of conflict with Spain.

However, there are other longer-term consequences that could have been included to improve it still further. The answer could develop arguments about the long-term consequences of the defeat of the Armada. These include:

- its impact on Elizabeth's historical reputation as a monarch
- its impact on naval warfare tactics
- its impact in laying the foundations for England's future as a global superpower.

## OVER TO YOU

Use pages 82–85 to help you write another paragraph about the long-term effects of the Armada's defeat.

Ever since Elizabeth became Queen, relations between England and Spain were tense. The Spanish King, Philip, had been married to Mary Tudor and resented losing his influence over England. He was also angry that Elizabeth rejected his marriage proposal. The Spanish tried to destabilise Elizabeth by encouraging Catholic plots involving Mary, Queen of Scots. These schemed to make Mary Queen and to assassinate Elizabeth. Meanwhile, English privateers such as Francis Drake raided Spanish treasure ships, gaining wealth for the nation.

The long-term tensions between England and Spain erupted into outright war in the 1580s which threatened England's independence and Elizabeth's position as Queen. The Spanish Armada appeared to have all the advantages, but their plan to invade and conquer went badly wrong. Drake's master-stroke was to use fireships against the Spanish fleet whilst it was anchored at Calais. The Spanish panicked, broke up their strong crescent formation, and they then lost the subsequent Battle of Gravelines.

The defeat of the Armada boosted English national pride, and Spain was left humiliated. Elizabeth, who had made a rousing speech to her troops at Tilbury during the crisis, was able to use the Armada for propaganda purposes. It boosted her popularity enormously and the 'Armada Portrait', one of the most famous pictures of Elizabeth, was painted to celebrate the event. However, the costs of the war also put strain on the economy, causing inflation and great poverty for the English people.

### Question 4

Question 4, which carries the highest marks, is an essay question based on a specific place (a historic environment) such as a palace, a manor house, a theatre or a battlefield. For example:

> 4. The main change to Elizabeth's royal residences was not the buildings but the way she used them.
>
> How far does a study of Hampton Court Palace support this statement? (16 marks)

Your aim is to use your knowledge of the period to connect this site (its features and its significance) to the wider developments you have studied in the rest of the depth study. You will be told what the site will be in advance of the exam and you will have studied it thoroughly. However, you will not be told the specific aspect of it that the question will focus on. You will be given a statement about the period which connects to the site and you will need to write an extended essay using your knowledge about the site and about the period to show how this statement is true. You need to know your site well to write an essay but, equally you also need to think clearly because the best answers will be those that develop a clear, coherent and relevant argument from the start, and carry it through the whole essay supporting the argument.

The key thing to remember about question 4 is that it is inviting you to reach a judgement – agreeing or disagreeing with the statement and using the site to support your answer.

The most striking thing about Elizabeth's reign is that her royal residences did not change much even though there was massive architectural change elsewhere in the country. However, the way Elizabeth used them changed a lot because she was a woman, and because she used progresses and spent long periods away from her own residences.

This is a great short introduction. It addresses the question and gives the reader a clear idea of the writer's final conclusion.

Elizabeth's father Henry VIII had spent a lot of money extending and rebuilding Hampton Court Palace to impress visitors. This was to reinforce his power. Foreign ambassadors and nobles would be received at the Palace, and would be impressed by the grand scale of the buildings. It contained hundreds of rooms to provide accommodation for the Court and visitors, and the vast kitchens were equipped to feed the members of the Court. The grand state apartments were designed to impress. The Great Hall, for instance, is a vast and hung with priceless tapestries.

You could extend this with details about:

- Who built Hampton Court Palace?
- How did it come to be a royal residence?
- What was the Palace built of?
- What were its main design features?

In reality, however, all that could have been said about the Palace in Henry's reign. The building itself was hardly changed by Elizabeth. It was the way she used it that changed. Mostly she used it as a country retreat – with easy access to London. But England in Elizabeth's reign was a 'personal monarchy', so the place where Elizabeth lived was of enormous importance politically. When Elizabeth was at Hampton Court people flocked to the Court to be close to the Queen, to gain power and wealth. Political scheming was rife. Elizabeth liked to keep the nobles close to her, so that she could monitor their behaviour and play different factions off against each other. The Palace's private rooms were therefore just as important as the grand public ones. Elizabeth was quite manipulative and the design of the Palace as a series of rooms which became more and more private as you proceeded through them meant that access to the monarch could be strictly controlled.

By Elizabeth's reign Hampton Court was not an impressive place, but an out-dated building. Unlike previous monarchs, Elizabeth did not undertake any major building works either at Hampton Court or any of her other residences. This was because she was short of money. In contrast, Elizabeth's subjects were building impressive 'prodigy houses' in the latest styles, where Elizabeth would often stay on her summer progresses. Elizabeth cleverly moved around the country on these progresses with her Court, staying in the houses of her subjects. She partly went on progress to save money. The progresses had a very positive effect though as they made Elizabeth highly visible, and she impressed her people through her clothing, style and wit. This made her stronger and more popular.

Most importantly then, Elizabeth used her personality to maintain her power, rather than using the buildings she lived in. Therefore, Hampton Court was really only important when she was actually there. When she was elsewhere, it was irrelevant. She understood that to be a strong and successful monarch, she had to be a good performer – almost like an actress. She was very careful to use lots of propaganda to craft an almost mythical image of herself, whether this was through portraits, plays or poetry. At Hampton Court the Great Hall provided a space for entertainments such as masques and plays which, as well as being impressively sumptuous, also contained subtle political messages to strengthen Elizabeth's image.

In conclusion, Hampton Court Palace itself had been impressive and important earlier in Tudor times. It was no longer so by Elizabeth's reign. It was an old-fashioned and neglected building in her time. The main change it demonstrates is that power was now all about having access to the Queen – being close to her wherever she was.

The first sentence of this paragraph is a great signpost. It tells the reader that we've moved on to thinking about ways in which Hampton Court was used.

The rest of this paragraph is about how the Palace helped Elizabeth to rule the country. There could be more precise details about how this worked.

- Use page 18 to find out about patronage, the Privy Chamber and the Privy Council at the Court, and make a brief list of details that you could add to this paragraph.
- Can you name specific individuals at the Court? What factions existed?
- Can you explain how Elizabeth being a woman changed the way government worked?

You could extend this with details about:
- Why was Elizabeth so short of money?
- How was Hampton Court different to the latest fashionable prodigy houses being built by Elizabeth's subjects?
- Where Elizabeth went on progress

Can you spot the phrase that is used to tell the reader about the relative importance of this paragraph?

You could extend this with details about:
- Can you name some other royal residences Elizabeth used?
- How did Elizabeth use art, plays and poetry to cast herself in a good light?

This conclusion directly answers the question, by referring to the points in the rest of the answer.

## Keys to success

As long as you know the content and have learned how to think, this exam should not be too scary. The important things to remember are:

- Read the question carefully. This may sound obvious, but sometimes students answer the question they wish had been asked rather than the one that has actually been asked. So identify the skill focus (what they are asking you to do). Do they want you to write, an account or an explanation? Identify the content focus and select from your knowledge accordingly.
- Note the marks available. That helps you work out how much time to spend on answering each question. Time is precious. If you spend too long on low-mark questions you will run out of time for the high-mark ones.
- Plan your answer before you start writing. For essays this is particularly important. The golden rule is: know what you are going to say; then say it clearly and logically.
- Check your work. You will never have time in an exam to rewrite an answer but try to leave some time at the end to check for obvious spelling mistakes, missing words or other writing errors that might cost you marks.

### OVER TO YOU

Successful answers will focus on particular aspects of the site. Read through these points and see if you can identify where in this answer these things are covered. Which bits are missing and could be added?

- location, structure, and design
- the way the site was used
- people connected with the site
- how the site reflects culture, values and fashions of the Elizabethan period
- how the site links to important events and/or developments during the Elizabethan period.

# GLOSSARY

**ABDICATE**: When a monarch gives up their throne.

**ACCESSION**: The time when an individual becomes a monarch.

**ALLEGORY**: Writing or art containing metaphorical symbols that have hidden moral or political meanings.

**ALMS**: Charity given to the poor. Almshouses are houses provided for poor people to live in.

**AMBASSADOR**: The official representative of a foreign ruler at the Court.

**ARABLE LAND**: Land used for growing crops.

**ARMADA**: A fleet of warships.

**ASTROLABE**: An instrument used by navigators to calculate latitude.

**BEACON**: A fire set up in a high position as a warning. A chain had been built across England prior to the Armada.

**BROADSIDE**: A firing of all the guns from one side of a warship.

**BULL**: A decree issued by the Pope.

**BUREAUCRACY**: A system of government involving lots of departments and paperwork.

**BURGESS**: An inhabitant of a town or borough who represented that place as an MP.

**CALVINIST**: Protestant followers of John Calvin of Geneva.

**CENSORSHIP**: To block something from being read, heard or seen, usually by the government.

**CENSUS**: A population count.

**CHAPLAIN**: A clergyman attached to the private chapel of a prominent person.

**CIRCUMNAVIGATION**: To travel all the way around the circumference (of the world).

**CLERGY**: Churchmen, including priests, bishops and archbishops.

**COLONY**: An area ruled over by another country.

**CONSPIRACY**: A secret plan to do something unlawful or harmful.

**COURT**: The residence of the monarch and their household.

**COURTIERS**: Members of the Royal Court who attended and advised the Queen.

**CULT**: A system of devotional worship directed towards a particular figure.

**CULVERINS**: A type of cannon used on English ships that was light, easy to reload and had a long range.

**DEARTH**: When food is so scarce and expensive that it threatens famine.

**DEATH WARRANT**: An official order for the execution of a condemned person. It had to be signed by the monarch, then authenticated with the Royal Seal, and then delivered to the place of execution.

**DEBASEMENT**: To reduce the amount of precious metal in a coin.

**DYNASTY**: A ruling family.

**EMPIRE**: An extensive group of colonies ruled over by a single more powerful country.

**ENCLOSURE**: The division of land, including the village common land, into separate fields with hedges, allowing a change from arable to sheep farming.

**EPISCOPAL**: A Church hierarchy structured around bishops.

**EXCOMMUNICATED**: To be expelled from the Church.

**FLAX**: A plant used to make linen.

**GALLEON**: A large ship, especially used by Spain, either as a warship or for trading.

**GALLEY**: A type of ship with sails and oars.

**GAUNTLET**: An armoured glove worn by a soldier.

**GENTRY**: Well-born families who owned land, but did not have titles and so were below the rank of the nobility.

**GREAT CHAIN OF BEING**: An idea that everything in the universe had its place in a rigid hierarchy.

**HEIR**: The person who is next in line to inherit the throne.

**HEMP**: A plant that could be used to make rope.

**HERETIC**: A person who did not follow the official religion of the country.

**HOUSE ARREST**: The state of being kept as a prisoner in a house, rather than in a prison.

**HUGUENOT**: A French Protestant. They suffered severe persecution and many emigrated.

**HUMANISM**: Intellectual branch of the Renaissance, drawing on classical texts and stressing the dignity of mankind.

**ILLEGITIMATE**: The opposite of legitimate, meaning a child born out of wedlock.

**INFLATION**: Rising prices.

**JESUIT**: Roman Catholic missionary priests.

**JUSTICE OF THE PEACE**: A JP is a magistrate who heard minor cases in local areas.

**LEGISLATION**: Acts of Parliament (laws) had to be approved by the monarch and both Houses of Parliament.

**LOGGIA**: A gallery with one side opening on to a garden.

**MARTYR**: Somebody who suffers and dies for their beliefs.

**MASS**: One of the seven sacraments, re-enacting the last supper. A key Catholic ritual.

**MONASTERIES**: The religious houses occupied by monks, dissolved by Henry VIII between 1536 and 1540.

**MONOPOLIES**: Royal licences giving individuals sole right to sell or make a product, leading to their profit and often leading to high prices.

**MULLIONED WINDOWS**: Large windows made up of lots of panes of glass divided by vertical supports.

**NATIONALISM**: Patriotic feelings marked by a desire for superiority over other countries.

**NEW WORLD**: A sixteenth-century term for North and South America, newly discovered at this time by Europeans.

**OTTOMAN EMPIRE**: A Muslim empire centred on Turkey that was rapidly expanding at this time, extending across North Africa, Arabia and Eastern Europe.

**PATENT**: A licence that gives a person sole right to do, make, use or sell something.

**PATRONAGE**: Using wealth, power and influence to promote individuals who then owe their patrons loyalty.

**PEERS**: Members of the nobility sitting in the House of Lords.

**PERSONAL MONARCHY**: Where politics and government revolve around the monarch and their Court.

**PLAGUE**: The bubonic plague was a very infectious disease spread by rats and fleas. It caused swellings called buboes, fever and usually death. When it first struck Europe, it had killed about half the population and it was a recurrent problem in Tudor England.

**PLANTATION**: A type of colonisation involving the establishment of a government-sponsored settlement of emigrants.

**POOR RATE**: A local tax used to fund workhouses and poor relief.

**PRINTING PRESS**: Invented in the fifteenth century in Germany, it allowed the mass production of books and images.

**PRIVATEERS**: Pirates licensed by the government to attack and loot enemy ships.

**PRIVY COUNCILLORS**: Members of the Privy Council, the committee of ministers appointed to advise the monarch.

**PROGRESSES**: Royal tour visits to the homes of the nobility.

**PROPAGANDA**: Something that spreads a message in order to encourage people to think or behave in a particular way.

**PROPHESYING**: Prayer meetings where the Bible was discussed and sermons said.

**PURITAN**: An extreme Protestant, favouring very plain churches and simple church services without music.

**PURSUIVANTS**: Government priest-hunters who would search houses suspected of hiding Catholics.

**QUEEN REGNANT**: A queen ruling in her own right rather than because she is married to a king.

**RACK-RENTING**: Charging an extortionately high rent.

**RECOINAGE**: To stabilise the currency, old debased coins were melted down and new coins issued.

**RECUSANT**: Someone, usually a Roman Catholic, who refused to go to Church services.

**REFORMATION**: A movement for the reform of abuses in the Roman Catholic Church which ended up splitting the Church with the establishment of separate Protestant Churches.

**REGENT**: A person who governs on behalf of another who is incapable of ruling due to age, ability, illness or location.

**REGICIDE**: The deliberate killing of a monarch.

**RENAISSANCE**: An intellectual and cultural movement originating in Italy in the Middle Ages, heavily influenced by the Ancient Greeks and Romans.

**SACRAMENT**: A sacred ritual recognised as of particular importance.

**SCEPTRE**: an ornamental wand held in the hand of a ruling monarch at the coronation as a sign of their power and godliness.

**SEMINARY**: A school providing training for priests.

**SMALLPOX**: An often-fatal viral disease, the symptoms of which included fever and blisters.

**SUITOR**: A man who pursues a relationship with a particular woman, with a view to marriage.

**TAVERN**: A public house serving alcohol and food as well as providing accommodation for travellers.

**TRAITOR**: Somebody guilty of treason.

**TRANSUBSTANTIATION**: The belief that the bread and the wine used in the Mass turn into the actual body and blood of Jesus Christ.

**TREASON**: A crime involving disloyalty to your country, monarch or government.

**UNIFORMITY**: All being the same.

**VAGABOND**: A homeless vagrant, wandering from place to place, who would beg and steal.

**VAGRANT**: A homeless, unemployed person who wanders from place to place and begs.

**VESTAL VIRGIN**: In Ancient Rome there were six women who took a vow of chastity and whose lives were dedicated to the goddess Vesta.

**VESTMENTS**: The garments worn by the clergy.

**WATTLE AND DAUB**: Walls built from interwoven wooden strips covered in mud or clay.

**WORKHOUSE**: An umbrella term for the institutions set up by the Poor Law. Separate institutions were envisaged by the laws, but the distinctions between them became blurred over time. In theory, poorhouses were to provide shelter for the 'impotent poor', workhouses to provide work for the 'able-bodied poor', and 'Houses of Correction' were to detain the 'idle poor'.

**YEOMAN**: A farmer who owned his own small estate.

# INDEX